Journey into Fear

When the dot com bubble burst

By The Fly

Editing and Artwork by Eric Thompson

Prologue

Hi Baba,

George told me about his second book and I was so happy for him – I offered to write the prologue for him. People tell me the first book was really good and when I have some time, I am definitely going to buy it and read it.

George and I go way back to the late 90s, when I was trading my big guy and making millions. I got lucky and left the firm before the shit hit the fan (pardon my language) and then I did some other things that went really well.

I remember when George got kicked out of the office that he shared with me and how angry it made me when they put someone I didn't know next to me. George used to help me with ideas for my big guy and it was messed up that they kicked him out into the boardroom. I mean, they gave Abdul an office and he was such a piker.

These days, I spend my time running several insurance companies and I own a lot of real estate. About a decade ago, I got into commercial real estate in Brooklyn, right before prices took off, and I did really well in that. I built a new house near the water in Bay Ridge and did much of the construction myself. It's cheaper that way.

To be honest, I haven't seen George in about 15 years – but I heard he's doing well, even though he lost much of his hair and runs some finance site from somewhere in New Jersey. I never liked New Jersey – too many highways.

By the way, I once tried to start my own website at around the same time Amazon came out. I used to visit all of the store owners in Bay Ridge and ask them to mark down their items by 25%, so that I could sell it on my site. For a while, it did really well. But then it became too much of a hassle, so I gave it up.

Aside from real estate and insurance, I own 4 restaurants in Brooklyn and they're really, really good. You should come out some day to see me and have a glass of wine.

Take care and smile, ok Baba?

-Chris from Brooklyn

Chapter I

Our plans of grandeur and success were spoiled by the endless waves of late comers trying to grab a piece of the billions to be made on the internet. One moment we were immersed in a state of perpetual winship, embossed by the dreamers and their petards, then we were hoisted by them.

The Nasdaq reached an ebbtide after the first week of March 2000, stopped going higher, and then rapidly collapsed by 78% over the next 30 months of lecherous liquidations. None of us had game plans for if and when things went awry. We lived out our lives in a symbiotic manner with a rapidly changing societal landscape that was based on a fantasy -- blinded by the whirring haze of hedonism, greedily riding the stock market carousal until it ruthlessly sundered. After an 86% run in 1999 and another 35% in the first 3 months of 2000; we wanted more, not because it made sense or because it was justifiable, but because we were entitled to it. We were whimsical miracle makers, barreling towards perdition, in a car made of dynamite, racing towards the sun.

By March 20th, 2000, the violence of the market downturn was becoming troublesome, down ~9% over the past 6 trading days. Unlike previous market corrections during the dot com rise, this one felt different and it cast an immediate pall on the office.

My partner and I, Giovanni, were getting obliterated in our largest position, a company named Harmonic Lightwaves that was down 11% for the session, trading at $102. During the entire dot com run, Harmonic Lightwaves was a crowd favorite, fortunes were made off its meteoric rise – because they were supposed to change the world. Everyone was back then. We had just bought the stock a fortnight ago for an average cost of $135. Because we liked the stock so damned much, after we were fresh out of money from buying up shares, we borrowed more from a margin account and told our clients it would pay off in spades. This wasn't anything new for us or anyone trading tech stocks those days. We all used margin accounts – because we wanted to double our gains. After all, why make just $100,000 when you could make $200,000?

We had lots of other positions on the books, but our hearts were in this one. We truly believed in it and made sure all of our favorite friends and family members held it in size, leveraged to the hilt, for the richness of it -- because it was going to change the world.

It wasn't long before ungoverned greed morphed into hair on fire panic. Our positions were bombed into dust and our favorite friends and family members got annihilated.

The Nasdaq was lower by nearly 4% that day, yet losses in our stocks were far more unforgiving. People could not sell stocks fast enough, not just because they were scared, but also because they were getting wiped out.

"George, we've got to sell some of these cocksuckers, else the accounts are gonna get wiped out," said Giovanni to me with a face stricken by panic.

I replied, "relax, dude. This too shall pass. Let's make sure our clients send in more money to take advantage of the dips."

He replied, "you've got a few screws loose. We're gonna get wiped out!"

You could hear a pin drop in our office, as we watched our fledgling careers being flushed down the toilet. Only the intermittent beeping sounds of the computers broke the awkward silence as we sat there, gawking at the unbelievable specter of it all.

"For real," said Giovanni, "we really need to sell out of this shit. It's all fun and games until your accounts drop to zero."

I replied, "quit being so doom and gloom, old man. Very soon you will see the men separated from the boys. Watch and learn."

"If this is what it feels like to be a man, I'd prefer to be a woman," said Giovanni. "Look, we're down a solid 40% over the past week on leveraged accounts. At this rate of return, we'll be wiped out, clean, clean I tell ya, by next week."

Giovanni's hands were shaking more than usual that afternoon and his face started to blend in with the gray rugs on the floor.

"Let's just sell everything, George. I'm telling you, this market is toast. We're gonna have accounts getting pulverized if we don't sell soon. Plus --"

I interrupted, "sell now? Are you nuts? If we sell now and the market recovers, our clients are going to feast on our balls forever. Look, we've been through a lot of ups and downs the past two years. This is just like 1998. It won't be long until we're richly rewarded for riding this fucker out."

Giovanni's eyes were now darting all over the office. He said, "then let's just sell a little bit. These accounts are gonna all get margin calls tomorrow, so either clients send in more money or we're gonna have to sell anyway, whether we like it or not."

The more Giovanni panicked the more relaxed I became. I sometimes viewed him as a contrarian indicator, only because he was more cautious than I was, probably due to our big age gap. During the dot com run, betting against Giovanni's natural neurotic bearishness served us very well.

"I can get wires in tomorrow. Lee said he'll send in another $500,000, and a few other of our larger accounts said they wanted to add and buy the dips," I said.

"Lee is down by 50%, isn't he?"

"More or less."

A defiant Giovanni grabbed a stack of sell tickets that he had already written out and said, "well, I'm gonna sell out of these accounts now. They're below maintenance and Felicia is giving me shit about covering the margin calls. You can call some of our bigger guys and see if they'll send in more money."

"Suit yourself," I said. "The clients you're selling for now will be feasting on your balls tomorrow."

Giovanni ignored my dire warnings and ran out of the office, like a schoolboy at 3pm, and dropped off the sell tickets at an angry trading desk.

My assistant Kim called and said, "Keith called again and demanded that you call him back before the market closes."

Kim was the head sales assistant, overseeing a staff of 15, and Giovanni secured her fealty to us by bribing her with 3% of our monthly gross, which was three times the normal rate. With the $350,000 in commission we had in for the month, she stood to make $6,850 for logging our trades, answering our calls, and doing rote clerical work. His logic was that by securing her services, she'd make sure all of our stuff was done quickly, since she had pull with the hard-boiled managers and malcontents in the back office. I never wanted to deal with them, ever. Since we just got a boost up to a 65% payout from 60%, parting with 3% seemed like a reasonable investment at the time.

Keith was my most difficult client, an old oil man from Texas who hated everything but the Republican Party. Getting him to transfer his $300,000 account to me was easy, however. All I had to do was remind him how much he hated his broker, offer a logical solution, and then lure him with all of the gains I had been enjoying during the bull market. I got his account up to $450,000, without the use of margin. He always rebuffed my suggestions to leverage out his $450k to $900k. In his thick Texan accent, he used to tell me "I never borrowed a red cent in my entire life and I sure as hell ain't gonna start doing it now with some Yankee for stock purchases."

"Keith, it's George. Sorry I didn't get back to you earlier, I've been busy trying to douse the flames over here, but this darned gasoline isn't quite getting the job done. How are you?"

"Oh, you're real funny, George. I'll tell ya what in the hell else is also funny – me trusting you with all of my money, which, according to your little assistant there is only worth $350,000 now."

"Are you really bitching about being down 20% from the highs, Keith? Hell, I've got accounts down a lot more than that. You're practically up. After I get off the phone with you, I got to call my Mother and let her know she's nearly wiped out. Relax, you're fine."

"You sound like an even worse son than a stockbroker, something I didn't think was possible. Well, I don't feel fine, George. How's Pete doing? You know I feel awful about referring him to you, seeing that everything has gone to hell."

"Pete is fine, just like you – barely down 20%, living the life, getting fat off the land, waiting for the market to turn. Trust me, you're gonna be shining my God damned shoes and begging for my forgiveness when the market reverses higher."

"The hell I will, you son of a bitch. I'll tell you what I will do. I'm gonna give you one more chance, then I'm getting the hell out of there. You hear me, son?"

"Yeah, yeah, yeah. You've been saying that for the past year and every time I've proved you wrong. Right?"

"Well, we'll see about that George. Goodbye."

And he hung up.

Our calls always went like that. Most of the time he'd slam the phone down before I could finish my last sentence. I always got a kick out of our phone calls, probably a lot more than Keith.

Giovanni blew out of some minor positions that day, such as Autoweb, Onsale, Lycos, and GBT Telecom. I held clients in and raised hundreds of thousands of cold hard cash to cover margin calls, in order to keep the dream alive. It wasn't a difficult proposition, convincing people to keep their dreams alive. Most of the people I spoke to were sold on the idea that the drop was temporary and were glad to hear my confidence and were even happier to send me more money to hold onto their rapidly depreciating assets.

Markets rebounded the next day and for the remainder of the week, with the Nasdaq sporting impressive 8% gains. In spite of the market rebound, Harmonic Lightwaves finished the week flat at $102. With the market racing higher, I truly wanted a reason to mock Giovanni and call up Keith and brag about my genius – but I was denied this pleasure due to a late Friday plunge in the stock.

It was around this time that an old friend of mine that I once worked with joined the firm. His name was Chuck and he left the business at the lows in 1998 and missed out on the entire run up. Like a fool, he spent his days chasing girls, drinking heavily, and taking meaningless college courses just so he could chase more girls and drink even more heavily. He already had a college degree and wasn't seriously perusing graduate course work. The winter winds of the market crash of '98 sent Chuck into hibernation and I was glad he decided to wake up and come back to work.

Chuck was average height and build, with neatly cropped chestnut brown hair, pale skin, greenish-blue eyes, and a square jaw. Upon first impression, his school boy looks disarmed just about everyone who met him, until they got to know him better and saw what a devil he was. Like a wolf in sheep's clothing, Chuck used his boyish countenance to advance his sociopathic tendencies, one beset with violent fist fights in bars and an unbelievable solicitous lifestyle with members of the fairer sex.

One week prior to joining the firm, Chuck was enjoying the company of one of his lady friends at an upscale lounge in Midtown Manhattan. It was a dimly lit and spacious place, with dark furniture, dark walls, and a glowing bar showcasing an extensive collection of fine spirits. The people there were mostly professionals, all wearing fashionable clothing, taking in the decadence and fragrant smells that wafted through the rarefied air.

While Chuck was enjoying his usual vodka with club soda on the rocks, three rusticates interrupted the conversation he was having with his lady friend, attempting to woo her away with juvenile pick up lines and belittling Chuck.

"Hey, why don't you come over here and join us and get away from that loser? It's a win-win situation," said one of the three rusticates to Chuck's lady friend. Mistaking Chuck for a scared school boy, they pursued this line of harassment until Chuck said, "mind your damned business pal."

This drew jeers and consternation from the trio, laughing and decrying Chuck to be nothing more than a paper tiger.

"Oh, what are you gonna do, beat us all up?", cried one of the three.

A normal man might've grabbed the check and left with his date, but not Chuck and not on this night. He asked his lady friend to meet him at his apartment, telling her he had to "take care of some business" before he could meet her. Not thinking anything unusual about this request, she kissed him goodbye and he told her he'd see her soon.

He broke off from his female companion and settled into the darkest corner of this dimly lit and brooding lounge, fixed on his new enemies – waiting for an opportunity to strike. At only 5'10, 155 pounds, what Chuck lacked in brawn, he made up for in wit. Chuck's modus operandi was to strike hard and fast, especially when his enemy least expected it, especially when his enemy was not looking. He prided himself on being able to knock people out with just one blow, saying "if you hit them really hard and really fast, when they're not expecting it, there's no way they can recover."

I'd always argue that this was a dishonorable way to fight, calling it 'sucker punching' -- which I felt bordered on cowardice. All of the fights I had ever been in were fair ones and I hadn't been in a real fist fight since high school. Chuck didn't care about sentimentality and merely viewed his fights as a means to beat his enemies into submission, without absorbing any personal damage. He'd get into at least one fight per month and he never lost, except for the one time when a bongoed female, coming to the rescue of her boyfriend, nearly gouged out one of Chuck's pale eyes with her pointy stilettos. These wild gambits had taken a toll on him, even though he was just 25 years of age. Sometimes during altercations, his right arm would dislodge from his socket, rendering him defenseless; and this forced him to make hasty retreats from battle – until he was able to snap his arm back into place.

Like a wolf tracking his prey, Chuck watched his enemies closely, undetected, and moved on one of them when he broke off to visit the bathroom. Chuck moved through the crowd with purpose, gently moving obstacles out of his way, until he reached the bathroom.

The rusticate was alone, relieving himself from all of the beer he had been drinking, finding solace in the quiet safety of the very trendy lounge urinal. Chuck, seeing a supreme first strike opportunity, rushed upon this urinating man and rapidly bashed his head into the shiny black tiles in front of him, accompanied with the words 'oh, you're not so tough now, are you?' He then set upon him with a savage comportment, mounting atop of him and repeatedly punching his face bloody -- until his arm suddenly dislodged, causing him to exit the bathroom post haste.

Chuck made it outside into the cool and crisp New York City night air, and then he was quickly seized upon by the other two rusticates demanding vengeance. Being the sly dog he was, Chuck spotted a police partition nearby, and with his good left arm, he grabbed the triangle part and began swinging it at their heads, like a fierce wild man trying to stave off death. He nearly took off the head of one of his attackers when, luckily, two bouncers subdued his enemies, which provided sly Chuck with a great opportunity to take his dislocated right arm and make an escape.

As Chuck ran towards Fifth Avenue, unbelievably, the man who he just left for dead on the bathroom floor was quickly giving chase.

The bloodied face pursuer cried out to Chuck, who was about 20 paces ahead, "I used to run track, there's no way you're getting away with this."

Mortified by the gravity of it all, Chuck ran faster, hailed a yellow cab, and hopped in it. But before he was able to get in a word to the driver, the ghoulish specter of the bloodied face man from the bathroom floor materialized in the most heinous of ways. He ripped open the cab door and plunged into the front seat next to the driver -- and then unleashed a riot of profanities onto poor Chuck, who sat amazed and cow eyed, feeling as if he was living out a real life horror flick.

Always thinking fast and one step ahead of his adversaries, Chuck blurted out "pay no mind to this man's silly remarks. He is my boyfriend and we are lovers. We had a quarrel and, unfortunately, we got into a fight. Driver, please take us to the nearest hospital so that he might receive treatment."

The bloodied face man was incoherent and seething with rage. He flatly denied Chuck's claims and said "this son of a bitch beat the shit out of me while I was taking a leak in the bathroom. I've never seen this person before in my entire life. Take us to the police."

The cab driver looked at Chuck and then the injured man, and then Chuck again, hoping he could figure out what to do.

Chuck looked confidently into the cab driver's eyes and then turned to the bloodied face man and said "don't be silly, Johnny. I love you." He waived to the cab driver and said "please, driver, we must get to the nearest hospital now."

The cab driver complied and raced towards New York Presbyterian, all the while chaos and tumult was unfolding inside his car. At the first red light, swift footed Chuck darted out of the cab, blazing into the New York City lights and melted into the darkness of a sleepy side street. While Chuck was running, he peered back and saw the cab driver had stopped his adversary from giving chase, demanding payment for the ride. After a few blocks of running, Chuck collected himself near Rockefeller Center, tucked in his shirt, and steadied his hair. He then hailed a cab and ordered it to his upper west side apartment -- where he continued his date with his eager lady friend, wasting the night away over a bottle of wine and a quiet movie.

Chuck and I had an understanding with one another. We had similar backgrounds and childhood experiences and we never tried to screw each other over. Come to think of it, I was probably the only person Chuck never tried to screw over and we got along just fine. He was thoroughly amused by the timing of his departure from the market and re-entry and often joked about it when stocks suffered, telling me with a big grin planted on his face, "George, what a time I chose to get back into the business, eh?"

I tried to keep his spirits high with words of encouragement and reminders of my miraculous 1998 comeback. I'd say things to him like "hey Chuck, quit being such a bitch. You're being gifted a chance to restart your business at lower prices – just like I did in 1998." Or sometimes, "look here son, these markets are for buying, not crying, so get on the phone and make some damn friends, else I'll give you a good hard smack across your cheek and gums."

Afterhours, we'd sit around the office and listen to recordings of legendary Wall Street brokers closing unbelievable sales or our favorite Jerky Boys' pranks – which always got Giovanni riled up and in a splendid mood.

Seated next to Chuck were our coldcallers, Dean and Eric.

Giovanni and I used to run help wanted ads in the NY Times, in search for talented coldcallers. Each Sunday ad in the Times would net us about a dozen responses, most of which were disappointing. But Dean distinguished himself from the moment we spoke to him. He was a darn good salesman and had the gift of gab. After he came in for an interview, we were so impressed with Dean, stupidly, we agreed to pay him double the going rate, or $600 per week. We only did this because Dean had promised to open 10 accounts per month; he even guaranteed it.

He said, "if I don't open 10 accounts by the second month of employment, you can fire me."

That seemed fair enough, plus the firm was covering half of our expenses.

Dean was a tall athletic looking man of 26 years of age. On his tanned face was a square jaw, sharp nose, and dead black shark eyes -- topped off with a healthy mane of shiny black hair. He had been in the business at another firm, working as an account opener under a senior broker for the past two years. He told us his broker got fired and he opted to part ways with him because he needed a change. Deep down, we both knew this story was bullshit, but we accepted it because we liked the idea of Dean opening up 10 accounts per month for us, guaranteed.

Eric was one of my best friends growing up and had been sanding floors before he came to work for me. We met each other on the first day of school in the 2nd grade, after an unfortunate incident which included him urinating his pants while sitting at his desk. Crying and wet from the immense amount of urine he just released onto himself, Eric stood up from his front row desk, pointed at me in the last row, and said "I want to sit with him." The next day of class our teacher moved me next to him and he never urinated himself again.

Eric was short, athletic looking, in spite of being a horrible athlete, with maple blonde hair, a long nose, and bright blue eyes. Growing up, he was liked by everyone and was very popular with the ladies. Even though we were the same age, he always looked up to me like an older brother and now I was going to teach him how to get rich in the stock market.

His father led a successful career on Wall Street as an executive at a major banking institution. After I hired Eric, he got his father to open up a $100,000 trading account with me – which was 'fuck you money' to him and probably done as a sign of appreciation for taking Eric under my wing.

Chuck, Dean, and Eric sat directly outside our office, in a little nook that was mostly unknown to everyone else at the firm. We were hidden back there and this allowed us to act like fools most of the time – fraternizing over alcoholic beverages and Giovanni's loud rap music.

Chuck and I started in the business at the same brokerage firm, which instilled the strictest of sales disciplines, and made sure everyone was working all day long. I never asked him to watch over our callers – but he did it anyway, probably because he enjoyed bossing them around.

On Monday, March 27th 2000, the Nasdaq was flat – but my Harmonic Lightwaves was careening lower in the most miserable of ways – off by ~10%, forcing dozens of our accounts into margin calls. Later that afternoon, the head margin clerk at the firm, a stern-faced woman with blazing red hair named Felicia barged into our office.

"What the fuck are you doing with these accounts?" pointing to two pages of margin calls that needed immediate cash infusions or liquidation.

Giovanni quickly responded, "hey Felicia, how are you?"

"Fine", she responded. "What are you doing with these accounts?"

He replied, "Don't worry, we'll be selling before the market closes."

"The hell we will," I said. "What if we decided not to sell and just hold until tomorrow, hoping for a little market appreciation to cover the calls?"

"What appreciation?", she raged. "Look, I don't have time for this shit. Either you get wires in pronto or sell out these accounts to cover the calls – else I will do it myself with market orders. I'm sure you won't like that."

Felicia stormed out of our office and Giovanni and I quickly made sure to cover all of our calls before the end of the day. We were both very scared of her. She did not get nor appreciate my sarcasm.

The idea of having to blow out of such fine stocks at such miserable discounts was hard to reconcile. Just a short while ago, the market was celebrated by one gigantic merger after the next: AOL and Time Warner, Broadcast.com and Yahoo, Geocities and Yahoo, in addition to dozens of others. How crazy was it back then? A CBS backed start up called iWon was giving away millions of dollars to people for simply logging onto their website.

The ebullience of excess was bountiful and you saw it everywhere.

"They have to come back," I muttered to myself.

The new economy was going to connect billions of people around the world, opening up commerce and efficiencies that were previously thought to be impossible. Clearly, people were panicking and once the dust settled, we'd be back to normal again and I'd be praised as a fucking hero for enduring through tough times. I viewed everything as a struggle, a cosmic game of the Gods, designed to test my mettle.

Giovanni was 14 years older than me and didn't give a shit about technology revolutions or the new economy; he only wanted to make a bundle of money and avoid being wiped out by rough downturns. Being a lot younger and reckless, I tended to view his bearishness as a confirmation to buy more – a grizzled outlook that was destined to fall by the wayside to a new world being created by entrepreneurs and young innovators.

Nevertheless, I went home that night feeling sick to my stomach, worried about the future and the legacy I was so desperate to create. I got home around 11pm, which was typical on busy nights, and my wife was doing the dishes. Jackie couldn't care less about the stock market and felt the industry was filled with a bunch of crooks and perverts. I'd often complain to her about my troubles, but I knew she'd rather discuss how little George's day went. She was a wonderful mother who sacrificed a teaching career and a social life in order to stay at home with our son – catering to his every whim.

"How was work hun?", she asked.

"Miserable. Fucking stocks crashed again and my accounts got killed."

"George! Please don't use that sort of language in the house. Little George might hear it and I don't want him exposed to that."

"You're right, sorry. Hey, I'm probably gonna have to work late hours at least 3 days per week again, since everything is getting blown to smithereens. We'll be needing some new clients to earn a decent living. All of my present accounts are down too much to trade or charge a lot of commissions."

"Whatever. You're hardly home any way. It's not like it'll make much of a difference. You really need to spend more time with George."

Whenever I argued with Jackie, I got flustered and stammered through the debates, often coming out a loser. She'd shoot down all of my ideas about work and success and made me feel like a morally reprehensible bad father, while at the same time serving me a wonderful dinner with a bright smile on her face and cheerful disposition.

"Jackie, what do you think I'm doing at work?", I said defensively. "I'm not having fun with friends, going out drinking and fine dining. I'm calling clients, prospects, getting hung up on all day, trying to build a business. Geez."

"Whatever George," said Jackie dismissively. "Last week you came home drunk and went out with your friends, so don't tell me you never go out."

"Oh, come on, I rarely go out – but sometimes I need to unwind."

"That's very nice George, I'd like to unwind too – but you don't see me doing that, do you?"

Feeling like a liar and a fraud, I attempted to defend myself again – but it was a futile endeavor. There was my version of events, her version of what those events might've been, and then the truth.

My work was sacred to me and I loved doing it – but Jackie hated it and that created tension that might've been avoided providing we had a more mature relationship. Her frustration was understandable, since she bore the responsibility of raising our son, while I was out working late hours, sometimes coming home with the stench of beer, asking "what's for dinner?" at 11pm.

Jackie was drop dead gorgeous, petite, and well liked by everyone who met her. People gravitated to her for her innocent charm and beauty. Raised by conservative South American parents, Jackie was a moralist and truly lived the life she preached, mostly good and honest – rarely doing anything that might be remotely considered to be impolite or untoward. I, on the other hand, had a different upbringing and often blurred the lines between good and bad, always aggressive and eager to win. But she kept me straight and honest and called out my bullshit when I was spinning it – and she hardened me to eschew self pity and excuses for failure.

The freedom inherent with youth was stripped away from us when we decided to have a baby at such a young age. Neither of us had family who could be called upon to babysit and we didn't trust nannies, so all of the pressure of raising our son rested heavily upon our shoulders.

For the remainder of the week, markets dropped dead on heavy volume. The Nasdaq plunged by ~8% and Harmonic Lightwaves bled out a horrifying 28%, closing on Friday at $83. It was the last trading day of March, a month that began with exuberant celebrations at the office, highlighted by high fives and cartoonish champagne consumption. During the first 10 days of the month, Giovanni and I recorded $350,000 in commissions -- our best month ever – now we were staring down the barrel of a gun.

On that final day, I capitulated, marking a poetic bookend to my ebbtide, selling out of most of my positions and reducing margin debt to almost zero. I was gobsmacked by the rendering and felt a deep sense of dread, staring at a moneyline that had just shrunk by 55% in a little more than a fortnight. The illusion of redemption, the chance to make things right, had slipped away and replacing it was the stark reality of loss, sorrow, and ruin.

"Don't worry George. We stopped the bleeding. We had no fucking way of knowing this shit was going to happen. Our clients know and trust us and will give us another chance to make things right. Cheer up," said Giovanni with a fraternal cadence.

I felt like I had been in a bad fight and got hit in the head too many times. Dazed and tired, I glanced over at Giovanni and said, "no that was it pal. We fucking blew it. I blew it. We should've sold last week when you wanted to and now we have cataclysm. I zeroed out Jackie's parents account, my mother is down 80%, and I feel rotten."

"We both messed up buddy. We're young and ambitious. We'll be ok. How much was Jackie's parent's account worth anyhow?

"About 5 grand," I said.

"That's chicken scratch George. Same thing happened to my jerkoff brother and I just wrote him a check and made him whole. Besides, we'll be taking home about $60,000 a piece this month. You can afford to just write them a check, no?"

"I guess so," I said while looking over my account pages, assessing the unbelievable damage.

Giovanni wondered, "how's your personal account doing? I know you've been really aggressive with it recently."

"More of the same, down 60% to around $325,000. It was heading towards a million just a few weeks ago. Now I don't even look at it. I expect to lose $10-20,000 a day."

Losing the money came so easy and required no effort on my part. "It wasn't real money," I thought. It was just numbers on a screen that jumped around wildly, meandering between greed and fear.

With an expression of deep concern, Giovanni placed his hand on my shoulder and said, "don't worry George, we'll make it all back and will be cutting dicks off in no time at all."

Chapter II

On the morning of Monday, April 3rd, 2000, I woke up thinking stocks might climb higher, but, instead, traders were burned at the stake and left for dead – led by the tech heavy Nasdaq which barreled lower by a clumsy 7.64%. Whatever remnants of joy that we had left in us was extinguished and replaced with acrimonious hatred for the markets, the job, and the entire world. I felt like the star of my very own Greek tragedy, tortured on a daily basis, humiliated at least once per week.

While liquidating all of our accounts on Friday, a few of them slipped through the cracks and we neglected to sell them out, including one that was heavily margined and approaching zero. He owned Harmonic Lightwaves and it was down an appalling 13% for the day.

Around 4:30pm Giovanni limped into the office looking like a yellow phantom.

"What happened, you look like absolute shit?", I asked.

"I just got back from a meeting with Felicia and Dave. Remember Jim's account, the one nearing zero? Well, we forgot to sell him out on Friday and now the account is in negative territory. Felicia just sold out the account in the after hours."

Not yet grasping the severity of the situation, I queried, "so how bad is it?"

"Negative $50,000. Dave said to call the client to cover the hit, otherwise it's on us."

"Holy shit. We have to cover the loss?"

"The firm sure as hell won't do it. They said we could work out a payment plan, maybe take $10k per month for 5 months until it's paid off. But I'm gonna call him now and see if he could send it in."

The thought of calling someone and asking for $50,000 just to get back to zero was a terrifying proposition and I wanted no part of it. I was glad Giovanni wanted to take responsibility for this task and wondered how he might do it.

"What sort of sales pitch could he make?", I thought intensely. I played out a few scenarios and they more or less went like this: "Hi Jim, sorry we completely fucked up. Hey, by the way, we didn't sell out your account on Friday, because the tickets got messed up. It's a messy, messy business over here – I'll tell ya. Hey, by the way, you wouldn't happen to have $50k lying around that you could send over, do you? We have a negative equity situation here that it's causing the firm to panic and we'd really like to avoid paying for it out of pocket."

Quite honestly, this was a job designed for the primordial, old testament Giovanni, a brash man who didn't know what the word 'no' meant. He could not relate to the average man who didn't want to send in $50,000 to get back to zero. "Giovanni was born for this very moment – the negative equity situation that menaced over us," I thought.
He rolled up his sleeves real high, grabbed the phone by its neck and choked it tight, roughly dialed some numbers into the phone, and got Jim on the line.

"Hey Jim, how are you?"

"Doing fine, Giovanni. How's the account doing?"

"That's what I am calling you about. We took a bit of a loss today, but I believe this is the moment we've been waiting for. General Patton once said, 'courage is fear holding on a minute longer'; I need you to trust me one more time and send in $250,000. I have a plan."

"I don't know, that's a lot of money. We already lost a good deal the past month," said Jim.

"That's correct, Jim. But, it was just three weeks ago when you and I were out to dinner celebrating the gains. We are going to have those times again – but I need you to step up today and send in the money. After the market rallies, I'll send back the principle and just invest the gains. You have my word. Okay?"

After a moment of contemplation, Jim said, "sure. I'll send in a wire tomorrow morning."

He never even told him the account was negative $50k. Had Jim said no, Giovanni would've told him – but he felt that the best way to raise the money for the loss was to ask for a lot more than was needed, trying to sell the idea of buying into an oversold tape. It was a masterful sale, one that shall forever be remembered in our small corner of the world.

"Yes, I fucking did it," Giovanni cried, high fiving me with animalistic vigor. "The wire will hit tomorrow. I'll invite Jim to dinner next week after he gets back from Vermont so we can go over the details."

Amazed by what I had just witnessed, I told him, "I am going to carve a statue with your likeness and attach the biggest set of balls the world has ever seen onto it."

"Thanks buddy, I really appreciate it," said Giovanni.

Dave walked in looking like a funeral director. You could tell the market was taking a severe toll on him and he was probably taking to the bottle every night to wash away all of the vile memories that were piling up.

"Don't worry Dave. I just got off the phone with the client and he agreed to wire in $250,000 in the morning. Tell Felicia not to worry."

"Oh, thank God. For a second there I thought you boys were finished. This fucking market is going to wipe us all out. I remember the crash in '87 and this feels just like that, only stretched out over many days, instead of one. Make sure you call all of your clients to tell them what the heck is going on. The fastest way to get slapped with a lawsuit is by ignoring them when they're losing money."

"That's good advice Dave," Giovanni said. "We're gonna call everyone tonight and give them a pep talk."

We called everyone that night, even the smallest accounts. It was important to remind people that we were human beings with families, aspirations and feelings, and not just Wall Street scum. Most of our clients were too shocked to fully accept the reality of the situation and were grateful to pick our brains and hear our theories. No one knew what the hell was going on – but we tried our best to keep spirits and expectations high.

Stocks recovered a bit in the latter part of the week; but we had little exposure to the market by then. Our apology tour was almost complete and we were anxious to move onto the next phase of rebuilding. Gone were the days when we could charge $3,000 on a $100,000 trade; we were doing trades for 100 bucks and felt bad taking that much.

That Friday we left the office late, almost 9pm. As we locked our office door, frazzled and threadbare, Giovanni turned to me gravely and said, "It's all fun and games until your account goes to zero." We then headed out into the brisk New York City streets completely unhinged and rudderless.

The next day my good friend Chris came to visit me at my house. He lived a few blocks away and liked to keep in touch so that he could update me on his wonderful life. After enjoying years of uninterrupted success, Chris left the firm in January of 2000, opting to start a hedge fund. He had one whale of a client with $10 to $20 million with him and big dreams for opening up a "trading floor for regular people", as he liked to call it.

He told me he had taken office space on Fifth Avenue in Bay Ridge and was going to fill it with dozens of computers and fancy coffee machines, catering to day traders who'd pay him for the pleasure of being able to trade stocks in an office environment. What Chris didn't seem to acknowledge was the fact that the world had been destroyed recently and no one had money to invest any longer.

"I think people would love to trade their accounts in a nice office with other traders. Don't you think so, Baba?"

"Well, maybe," I said. "But aren't you worried about the market being down?"

Chris laughed and rubbed his fat stomach and said, "Baba, this is just a correction. The market will come back, don't worry."

It was comforting to know there were people out there like Chris, seemingly immune to all of the pangs of misery that had plagued the rest of us on a daily basis. Nevertheless, it was obvious to me then that Chris had lost his mind.

"Say Chris," I said, "how much did you spend on this trading room?"

"Not much, maybe $100k. Enough about business, how's the family, Jackie, little George?"

"Not bad, everyone is still alive. How about you, Mom good?"

"Everyone is good. I'll tell her you asked about her. Hey, before I go, let me show you something."

He placed what looked like a face down check on my round glass table and said, "are you ready?"

"Yep, I'm ready. Let's see it."

Excited like it was his first day in kindergarten, Chris flipped the check over and it was $400,000, payable to him.

"What the fuck is this shit?", I asked.

"My first check since opening my fund. We agreed to quarterly fees, 20% of profits."

"Holy shit. You just got paid $400,000 for three months of miserable work? Aren't you down now? Please tell me you're down like the rest of us."

"Yes, but I went to cash right after the market got hit in March. By the end of March, I still had $2 million in profits, so this is my cut. Since then, I've been getting killed."

"Wait, are you down at all, or still up $2 million?"

"We're down a little Baba. I was a little scared they wouldn't want to pay my fees, but they did."

"Oh, lucky you," I said.

Chris had a permanent smile on his face, and for good reason. His life was perfect.

"So, what are you gonna do with the money, buy stocks?"

"Fuck no. I'm not touching this market," said Chris, unusually animated. "I'm going to buy a few houses around here and rent them out."

Even though Chris had been making six figures for the past 4 years, he still lived with his parents, saving up all of his money. Now he was going to buy a few houses and live in none of them. This made no sense to me. Then again, I wasn't Chris, a man who won the lottery every single day.

Chris looked at his watch and said, "hey Baba, it was good seeing you. I have to go meet the tech guy who is setting up the trading office in 15 minutes."

"When are you opening?"

"Probably in early May. You should definitely swing by and check it out."

"Definitely."

With a twinkle in his, Chris said, "everyone needs friends Baba. Send my love to Jackie?"

"Will do," and he left.

Shortly after, Jackie came home with little George and I told her about Chris's trading room idea and how he was going to buy two homes and still live with his Mother.

"Pretty crazy, right?", I said to Jackie, fully expecting her to agree with me.

"I think it's smart. Why don't we buy a rental house too? We have the money now and the stock market isn't doing anything, right?"

"Well, that's true, it's really not doing much of anything, really boring me to death; but I don't want to buy a rental house now. I know how to make money in stocks and don't know the first thing about investing in real estate. Plus, I'm too busy to start now."

"But real estate is stable and won't drive you crazy like stocks," she said.

"They don't drive me crazy, Jackie. They drive me nuts, but I love them – just like you."

"Oh, please George. I know you're just giving me the run around. You should learn a thing or two from Chris. He knows what he's doing."

Boy was she right, but I didn't want to admit it then.

I thought of something witty to say to her and then changed the subject.

Jackie didn't know the severity of my troubles. Hating my job the way she did cut both ways. I was conditioned to avoid talking to her about my work because I knew she wasn't interested and it'd just cause an argument. She felt Wall Street was a denizen of scoundrels and scam artists, which was mostly true, except for a few. I liked to consider myself a moral person, someone who wanted to do good and make a positive impact on others. But after the recent losses, I felt like all of the other frauds and scammers that Jackie had been telling me about for the past two years.

As far as Jackie was concerned, there was no honor in being a stockbroker and she'd make sure to tell little George about her feelings whenever the subject was broached.

While in bed that night, I remember looking up at the crown molding of my high ceilings with the fan moving slowly -- which cast an eerie shadow projected by the occasional passing car -- wondering about the different ways I could turn things around. I could calculate numbers in my head like a machine and was able to quickly reconcile a budget or balance sheet in seconds. When I had nothing, there was hope of making something. Now that I had everything, I feared losing it all.

Chapter III

Another problem the market had was the Federal Reserve. They seemed to think everything was wonderful and made an effort to ignore every market plunge and remind us how fantastic the economy was and how they needed to slow it down by raising interest rates.

Fourth quarter 1999 GDP came in pistol hot at +6.9%, which was the highest level since 1987. Reacting to what we all viewed as old news, on March 21st, 2000, the Fed hiked rates to 6%, which was the 5th increase in the past 8 months. Interest rates were now at the highest level since 1995, all the while stocks careened lower in true broken elevator fashion.

The head of the Federal Reserve, Alan Greenspan, said he wanted to orchestrate a 'soft landing', which was doublespeak for trying to slow the economy and mess up the market. Most analysts and pundits on Wall Street viewed these hikes as 'non-events', minor burls in the wood that could easily be smoothed out by the unprecedented innovation and growth taking place in the economy at the time. Although inflation has been virtually non-existent, with CPI registering just 2.2% for all of 1999, the Fed was hell bent on 'reigning in' speculation.

Two weeks into April and everyone at the firm couldn't stop talking about Greenspan and how much they hated him. They blamed him for everything, even the bad weather. Whenever a pundit on CNBC would defend Greenspan, calling Fed policy a 'non-event,' you'd hear a storm of four letter words directed at the television, like angry sports fans at a bar trying to desperately offer advice to an inanimate object.

Markets took a truly hellish turn for the worse that week, starting off with a 5.8% drop in the Nasdaq, followed by a 3.1% drubbing the next day. On Wednesday, stocks accelerated to the downside again, with the Nasdaq getting ransacked for a whopping 7%. Respite was not granted on Thursday, as we were hit for another 2.4%. On Friday, markets truly crashed, with the Dow dropping more than 600, triggering circuit breakers, sending the Nasdaq nosediving by 9.6% -- marking the largest point decline in history.

I fucking hated that week with all of my guts.

The frustration in the boardroom was beyond anything you could imagine. Well dressed educated men and women transmorphed into screaming animals, behaving like craven barbarians marooned on an island without any food.

When markets crashed on October 19th, 1987, the Dow had dropped by 22% in a single day, which prompted the newly appointed Greenspan to issue the following statement.

"The Federal Reserve, consistent with its responsibilities as the nation's central bank, affirmed today its readiness to serve as a source of liquidity to support the economic and financial system."

Greenspan followed up that statement by injecting $12 billion of 'high-powered money' into the banking system, buying government securities, providing liquidity to a panicked market. It worked like a charm. Once in the system, at a 10% reserve requirement, banks could generate $120 billion in new magic fiat money. This resulted in a 75bps plunge in the Fed funds rates and halted the market decline dead in its tracks, saving the economy from an almost assured tailspin.

But now, with stocks down 34% since March 10th, mired in a calamitous bear market, the Fed wasn't doing a damned thing. As a matter of fact, they kept issuing statements about 'inflation concerns' and how the economy needed higher rates, which culminated to that tumultuous drop on April 14th, 2000. We didn't need the benefit of hindsight to know that the Fed was completely and utterly detached from reality and were accelerating the violence of the rout.

After the circuit breakers shut down the market that Friday, my friend Paul came by to see me and asked if I wanted to get a beer. Eager to get the hell out of the stifling heat of my office and avoid thinking about the market, I agreed and walked out with him.

As I made my way through the office, I spied rows of downcast men with their faces planted in their hands, phones ringing off the hook and nobody answering them -- zombies glued to the television awaiting news. The office was a graveyard of wasted opportunity, the aftermath of excess and a reminder that to be young and filled with zeal didn't mean invincibility.

I wanted to drown my head in a stein of beer and get drunk enough to forget about my problems, and I did.

"Hey buddy, how are you dealing with this disaster?", I asked Paul.

Taking a deep breath, rubbing his tanned forehead just above his thin framed glasses, Paul said "I lost $15,000 in options today for my personal account. That was the last of it."

"You wiped out your whole account? Didn't you have like $200,000 in it like a month ago?"

"More like $300,000. Yep, it's all gone. I thought for sure we'd see a bounce today, instead it crashed and took out the rest of my account. It was my final gambit. I'm through George."

"Ah, cheer up. You'll get it back," I said. "Besides, who needs money when you have good cold beer like this?" We both clanked our steins together, nodded, then proceeded to guzzle down the contents of the large mugs without coming up for air. It was a silent contest often played by men, an intuitive reaction to a large mug of beer coupled with ample amounts of testosterone.

Wiping the beer scum from his face, Paul said, "can I borrow 10 grand?"

"Well, that was unexpected, but sure, why the hell not?", I said, with a near hysterical laugh. We then ordered two more beers and we started to feel a lot better about life and our prospects. It was a funny thing, the more we drank, the better things got.

There's an old saying that 'misery loves company'; and while I did not relish in the specter of seeing Paul agonizing over his losses, it did make me feel better. I wasn't the only one in pain. There were others, fellow soldiers injured on the field of battle, with similar wounds and feelings. We understood each other's pain, because we had been in the same war, one that was killing our dreams and turning us bitter.

Shortly after 5pm, Giovanni and the rest of the gang met up with us and we continued to celebrate like it was an Irish funeral. Overflowing steins of beer clanked high in the air, sloppily spilling its contents onto innocent bystanders below, just before being guzzled down until nothing was left. This continued for a few hours, then I excused myself, fearing Jackie's wrath.

"I'm gonna head out fellas. It's getting late," I said while looking at my watch.

A cockeyed Paul said, "ah, come on, quit being such a pussy, it's not even 7pm" slapping me on the back.

Giovanni, laughing and buoyant, grabbed Paul by the shoulders, giving him a brutally hard massage, said, "sure George, listen to this guy and you'll be single like him in no time at all. Get the fuck out of here to your wife and son. Let us losers waste the night away here, while you go do the right thing."

"Thanks Giovanni," I said. Before heading out, I told Paul that I'd give him a check on Monday for the $10,000 and then I left.

On the train ride home that night, I gazed out the window into the NYC subways as the train raced towards Atlantic Avenue, a horribly grimy and filthy station. It was a main transfer hub in Brooklyn and it was always very crowded, extremely dirty, and filled with an enormous amount of homeless men begging for money.

In the tracks were scores of rats the size of cats. During the summers, the sweltering heat was almost unbearable and trains were almost always late. It smelled like a smoldering fire and dust. The concrete floors were blackened from the heavy foot traffic, lined with dozens of metal beams that were painted firetruck red. When I was a teenager, my friends and I used to meet up there before heading to Manhattan. Outside the station was a major shopping district, but I avoided it because it wasn't a very good neighborhood and there were always fights and robberies outside.

After a short walk through the terminal, I transferred to the R train and was on my way home. While on the train, I couldn't help running numbers in my head, trying to project what my production numbers might look like for the month. I'd be lucky to generate $10,000 in commissions, a decline of 95% from our average in 1999. My personal brokerage account was down to $250,000 and I had another $175,000 in the bank. I thought about Chris and how his new trading office might be a nice place for me to hang out to trade my own account. I thought about taking all of my savings and investing it into the market – making a grand bet, just like I did in 1998. "Jackie wouldn't be very happy about that," I thought. But then I thought about all of the stories I read about people buying the 1987 crash and coming out the other end of it glorious, multi-millionaires with fireside stories to tell their grandchildren.

I was obsessed with the idea of building a legacy and I believed that risk was something to embrace, not avoid. Heck, Jackie just didn't understand. How could she? By the time the train stopped at my destination, I had made up my mind to truly get serious about trading my own account the following week.

On Monday, the Nasdaq rallied fiercely by 6.5%, and I sold out of my entire account, in order to have a clean slate. My final shares of Harmonic Lightwaves were sold at $57, down 60% from my original basis. I deleted the ticker from my monitor and vowed never to look at it again.

Giovanni stormed in holding a stack of papers that were flopping in his hand, excited like he just invented electricity, "I know what we're buying next."

Amused by his excitement, I said "whadda ya got?", with a big smile.

Like a man possessed, he said, "we're going back to the well. We're buying Qualcomm and we're gonna do it in size. I'm telling ya George. Take a look at these fucking charts." He then started to rifle through stock charts so fast that I could hardly see what they were.

He continued, "the stock broke a long downtrend today and bounced off an important Fibonacci level. I was going over the point and figure charts too and I think we could see the stock bounce 30% from here. If we buy a fuckload of the stock, margin it, we could make a good chunk of our losses back."

The phrase "going back to the well" often had a negative connotation for brokers. It meant he wanted to revisit a place where we had some recent success, hoping to repeat it. All real gamblers are superstitious; brokers were no exception.

"Giovanni, you never go back to the well. You know that. Sure, we had good times in Qualcomm, made a bunch of money in it before the 4 for 1 split. But aren't you worried about going back to the damn well?"

"Quit being a dick, George. I'm serious. Here, have a look at the point and figure chart. I'm telling you, it's gonna go."

Giovanni then showed me all of his charts again, this time more slowly, describing in great detail how the stock was going to trade for the next three months. He was like a sorcerer.

"George, see this resistance level here?", drawing a line across the chart with a pen and ruler. "The moment it breaks this line," repeatedly beating the tip of his pen into a section of the chart, "the stock is gonna fucking blast off."

I acquiesced to his supreme confidence and said, "sure, why the hell not? Let's fucking do it."

Giovanni shuffled his papers all about his desk, organizing them into neat piles, and then he rolled up his sleeves higher than usual, midway up to his biceps, and said, "I'm gonna start calling our clients now to give them the gameplan. You should do the same. Let's get as many orders as we can tonight and then drop these trades tomorrow. Ok?"

"Sold," I said.

Almost manic, Giovanni nervously dialed the phone and convinced everyone to buy Qualcomm. You could tell he needed that, a little bit of hope and optimism to break the bleak depression he'd been in. After each call, his face lit up and he looked at me with glowing approval and then filled out a buy ticket. By the end of the night, he had a thick stack of buy orders, maybe 50 or 60, maybe even more.

I did my part too, calling clients to provide them with good news and hope. I felt like I was offering passengers of the Titanic a lifeboat and they were all very excited to learn about my ideas and how this was going to spark a rally in their accounts, just like 1998.

Aside from that, I was, however, more focused on the idea of trading my own account.

"What am I going to buy?", I said to myself. Clearly, I wasn't going to buy Qualcomm – going back to the well was crazy and a jinx. I didn't need that in my life now. What I needed was a new idea that would pair nicely with my clean slate, something entirely different.

If Giovanni was right and Qualcomm ended up making our clients back 30% of their money, I'd be very happy about that. "But if I could snag a 100% winner for myself, that would be even better," I thought to myself with serious introspection.

Before heading home that night, I spent two hours on the Bloomberg terminal, scouring for fresh ideas. I finished my work around 10pm and made it home for dinner at 11:15pm.

I scanned though hundreds of stocks, trying to decipher charting patterns, and determined that I was going to buy JDS Uniphase. "This is it," I said to myself. I had found the stock that was going to make me rich.

The stock was up 23% during the previous session – and I thought it could go much, much higher. All throughout 1999, buying stocks into momentum was a great strategy to make gains. Giovanni used to say, "stocks in motion, tend to stay in motion."

I was going to bet on more motion and decided to buy 5,000 shares in the morning around $100, and then quickly sell it in a week at $120 or higher – at least that was the plan.

"If I'm right, I can make $100,000 for myself, which is the equivalent of doing about $400,000 in gross commissions," I muttered to myself.

Walking towards the train station that night, I felt like I had transcended the small, monotonous, world of money management. I wondered, "why bother running money for spoiled rich people when I could do it for myself?" I was going to be a whale, trading in Chris's new office, building my account into the tens of millions, laughing and popping bottles of champagne corks into poor Giovanni's face, as he toiled about the office with his point and figure charts. After making my fortune, I was going to retire and give Giovanni all of our accounts, and then travel the world with Jackie and little George.

On April 18th, 2000, excited about my new venture into actively trading my personal account for quick, spectacular, riches, I bought 5,000 shares of JDS Uniphase all at once. There wasn't any time for half measures or juvenile insecurities. This was a man's game, one wrought with harrowing dangers and financial insecurity; but I was well equipped to win, having perused the Bloomberg terminal for hours in search of the perfect stock.

I got filled at $98, a comfortable level for me, and was glued to the monitor for the balance of the day, watching every tick like a violinist reading the notes of a symphony. Simultaneously, Giovanni was buying large blocks of Qualcomm, getting clients all worked up over the prospects of 'making it back.' To make matters a little more complicated, our client Jim, the gent who just sent in $250,000 to dig himself out from a -$50,000 hole, was in the office, nervously watching his newly acquired position with Giovanni. I kept glancing over to them and was amused by the fact that they both looked like petrified children who were abandoned in a cold unforgiving forest with no means of getting home.

All three of us were gamblers fixed on our gambles.

Throughout the day, both Chuck and Paul barged in, asking me to go for a quick dalliance to lunch and sugary iced coffee – but I declined both invitations and didn't leave my desk until the market closed.

JDS Uniphase closed at $94, producing a wretched loss of $20,000 for the day. At the lows, the stock had hit $89, amounting to a $45,000 loss, which made me feel like raw meat going through a grinder. My head was spinning from the chaos and confusion. Giovanni and Jim were two grim looking fellows to my left, thanks to Qualcomm closing down 4% for the session.

All three gamblers had lost for the day. But there was always tomorrow, and the day after, and the day after that.

After the beating, I felt like guzzling down a few beers, so Giovanni, Paul, Chuck, and a good friend of ours, Nick, went to the local pub for a few.

I knew Nick from my previous firm. He had gotten fired for signing his own tickets, impersonating a manager. Other brokers at the firm began to think he was a manager too, since they saw him signing his own tickets, and it wasn't long before Nick was signing theirs too – until he got caught and was fired. Nick didn't benefit in any way from signing his own tickets; he merely did it out of sloth; and then he signed other brokers' tickets for amusement.

Nick had a strong face, dark features, and bright green eyes. He was always the center of attention, very garrulous, and liked to tell jokes. He was very laid back, a good listener, and was always seen laughing.

Because of his colorful persona, people sometimes mistook him for being gay; but Nick was used to that and I heard him tell people on more than one occasion, "no, sorry I'm not gay, umkay. I get that a lot, believe me, but I'm not gay."

Nights out during the dot com crash days weren't supposed to be fun, per se. They were more like funeral processions or therapy, with everyone sharing stories of stocks and clients that used to be alive, reminiscing over the good days of last month, and how we'd all been ruined in such a short time span. The bars were brimming with cigarette smoke and always had sticky floors. There was nothing uplifting about the pubs we visited and they were all very expensive – but they helped us forget, at least for a short while. We drank our sorrows away and began to feel better after 2 or 3 steins.

It was a pleasant scene, all young faces enjoying their youth, drinking excessively amidst the loud music and banter. Nick was laughing and choking on his cigarettes and Giovanni was making small talk with a portly bartender (who was also a client), while Chuck and Paul chased down some women. I was mostly a spectator and preferred to blend in.

Noticing I was by myself brooding, Nick came over to me and said "cheer up, huckleberry. Want a cigarette?", holding out a pack of Lucky Strikes with one hanging loosely from his mouth.

"No, I don't smoke. Thanks anyway."

"Bad day?", said Nick.

"You have no idea," I said. "Things keep going from bad to worse. I can't believe how fast we all got fucked."

Blowing loops into the air with his cigarette smoke, Nick said "fuck the market. It's always gonna disappoint. Know what I mean, jellybean? It's designed to beat us. We just got to make enough money from it and blow the fuck out. Start a new business or go live in South America and smoke weed all day."

"I hear what you're saying," I said. "That's easy for you to say, since you're single and ambiguously gay. But for me, I can't move the family down to South America and smoke joints all day."

"That's too bad. Who the fuck told you to get married so young anyway? What are you retarded?", said Nick sarcastically.

He continued, "you're fucked George. You ought to go back to the office right now and start cold calling." He then let out a very loud laugh.

I took a long sip from my beer and looked around the hazy pub for a few minutes and then glanced down at my watch and saw it was 7:45pm and felt bad that I was out so late with Jackie at home with little George.

I closed out my tab, said my regards, and hopped on the next train heading towards Brooklyn. I arrived home a little after 9pm – Jackie was upset because she could smell the smoke and the beer on me. No matter how hard I tried to explain to her that I needed to unwind, because I wasn't feeling well, she didn't understand.

She thought that if you drank alcohol because of hurt feelings you were an alcoholic -- and she told me that on more than one occasion. Jackie inherited her strong backbone from her mother and she didn't have empathy for any sort of frailty, with exception to old people and children.

At times, I resented the harshness of her rebuttals and accusations. Our giant egos would clash and cause riotous arguments – but we always made up and rarely held grudges. She'd threaten to leave me and I'd threaten to leave her; but at the end of the night, we'd sit down on the couch and watch our favorite shows together, eat late night snacks, and laughed a lot. We were best friends.

The only time Jackie ever walked out on me was over a cat.

On a cold and windy Valentine's Day night, we passed by a pet store and she fell in love with a beige Siamese cat, who had bright blue eyes, and was so small it fit into the palm of my hands. I bought her that cat on the spot for $1,200, in spite of never before owning a cat or knowing the first thing about the psychotic nature of the Siamese breed.

After 6 months, the cat was driving us up the walls. It'd howl loudly at night and attack us fiercely during the day. One of the cat's favorite victims was little George. The cat would perch itself on the couch and wait for George to walk by and then she'd pounce on him and scratch his face. Jackie felt the cat was a possessed demon and wanted to get rid of it right away. I viewed the cat like one of my stocks and didn't want to get rid of it – because it meant I'd realize a loss of $1,200. After weeks of bitter arguments over "Cathy the Cat", Jackie said to me, "me or the cat?" and I said, "well then, it's gonna be the cat," so she left to her Mother's house for the weekend.

During that time, we talked on the phone for hours like teenagers and she apologized to me and I apologized to her, and Jackie, of course, got her way and we got rid of the cat when she got back.

Chapter IV

The next three days felt like the worst days of my life. The Nasdaq slid another 8% and JDS Uniphase was all but routed. I was a fool on a fool's errand in search of fool's gold and I had found it. Capitulation was the buzzword and I joined the fray, selling out of that bastard of a stock at $80, locking in a $90,000 loss. To make matters inexorably worse, our Qualcomm position was crashing through the floorboards, down 9% on April 24th, 2000 – placing us in the red by ~11% from our basis.

I felt like punching myself in the face and jumping out of a window. Good thing our small office didn't have any, else I might've done it.

I didn't say a word to Giovanni, or anyone else, about what I was doing in my own account. Once worth $750,000, the measure of my success and my pride and joy, my tattered brokerage account was now down to just $160,000. Instead of recoiling from the danger, I raced towards it. Many years later, a good friend of mine accurately depicted my demeanor as thriving off the struggle, fighting like a rat trapped in a corner against phantom enemies, when in fact the only real enemy was myself.

In the weeks ahead, I feverishly traded my account, all but ignoring my business, my wife, and my son – casting aside all the financial canons and beliefs that once made me a great dot com trader. I was now a miserable gambler, diving into Sycamore from $69 to $61, Netapp from $69 to $58, Safeguard Scientifics from $49 to $44, Apple from $107 to $101, Time Warner Telecom from $59 to $45. EMC all but stole the show – nearly finishing me off with a horrifying ride from $132 to $107.

On May 23th, 2000, Dave barged into the office at 9:00am like a madman and said, "George, you forgot to sell out of your margin call yesterday, for your personal account. Felicia said she's gonna sell at the open, unless you write me a check now."

"How much is it?", I asked.

I could feel Giovanni's eyes on me, wondering what the heck was going on.

"Well, it looks like $14,000, but it might be more, depending on what the market does today."

I opened my desk drawer, cleared away a bunch of random staples and paper clips, and then produced a checkbook. I held it up to Dave and said, "I'll write you a check right now. Who gives a shit, right Dave? It's only money."

I wrote the check; Dave grabbed it and then looked down at me as I leaned back in my swivel chair and said, "let's hope this will cover it. You guys just don't learn, do you? I don't even want to know how much money you've lost in that account. But if you're gonna run a successful business, you can't let your personal account become a distraction."

Dave was filled with all sorts of cryptic warnings and life lessons from his years in the business. We always agreed with them, but rarely, if ever, did we heed his advice. We were young and virile, while he was washed up and wore a stupid mustache.

Instead of selling, I bought more stock that day, hoping to catch a quick day trade – but it ended in disaster. The Nasdaq was shattered by nearly 6% and I ended up losing the entire $14,000 I gave to Dave that morning, plus an additional $30,000. My account was down to just $15,000 and I was ashamed of myself. Before the market closed, I sold everything and bought bullish option contracts, betting for a quick move higher. It was the riskiest thing I could do – but it seemed like the appropriate course of action at the time – the final gasp of a cat drowning in a bathtub filled with goldfish.

On May 25th, 2000, I turned 24 years old, but I felt 40. The Nasdaq was down 36% from the highs, plunging scores of former high fliers into miserable and interminable declines. Our business was in crisis and I was on the verge of wiping out my entire brokerage account and Jackie didn't have the slightest clue of what I had been up to.

I woke up that morning and decided against going to work. I described work to Jackie 'like sitting in an electric chair all day, waiting for the executioner to give me the final shock' and I didn't want to do that on my birthday. She understood and I headed over to Chris's internet trading office, which was a short walk away from my house.

Chris greeted me outside of a Dunkin' Donuts, which was right next to his office. I grabbed an iced coffee from Dunkin' and then we went up to his place of business. It was a two story office, with rows of computers, none of which had been touched since he opened the place. It looked abandoned and sad, and all of the lights were turned off, probably to save on electricity. The morning sun crept through the trees and onto the light beige computer monitors, which gave the place a haunting aura. Even though everything was brand new, it felt old and doomed for failure. Chris didn't know the meaning of failure, so I doubt he would recognize the subtle signs around him; but I saw them everywhere.

We settled in his personal office, which was neatly decorated with diplomas and certificates, family pictures, and expensive wood furniture, wonderfully crafted.

"Any luck with this place yet?", I asked.

Chris, with a look of bewilderment, shook his head and said, "not a single person has come by, not even to look."

"It's a tough market buddy. I'm sure when things pick up again, this place will be brimming with degenerates. You have a great location and have done a great job renovating the place. Well done, truly."

"Thanks, I hope so Baba. This market has been killing me lately. My big guy is very nervous because we've been getting hit for $200,000 to $300,000 per day for the past week."

Chris and I watched the market that day, just like the old days when the world was falling part in '98. I listened to him try to calm his big client down, who was irate over his losses, and he saw me brooding over my trading catastrophe. As I watched my options go to zero, finally wiping my account out for good, it dawned on me that the last time Chris and I shared an office was at my lowest point in '98. Since then, I rose up and became the 3rd biggest producer at our firm, surpassing Chris by orders of magnitude. But there I was, racked and ruined again, at the lows, looking for some of Chris's luck to rub off on me.

He had run out of it himself, apparently.

That was the last time Chris and I shared an office. By the winter of 2000, he closed the office down, dashing his grand dreams of a comfortable place for internet traders to lose money for a fee, and then he lost his big client. He tried to trade his own account for a living, but got wiped out instead. Thanks to his timely real estate purchases, over time, he was able to recover and eventually he got into the insurance business, catching his stride again, and making millions in the process. Years later, Chris's big client called me and transferred what was left of his account, which was no more than $300,000.

After I left Chris's office that day, I went straight home and was delighted to be ambushed by a surprise party Jackie had planned for me. It was the first time anyone had ever done that for me and I was happy to see everyone's faces; but that happiness was checked by the gut wrenching grief I felt for blowing up my brokerage account.

A little later on that night, I told Jackie what I had done, and for the first time since my Grandfather passed away, I broke down in tears – talking fast and with extreme self-deprecation, fully expecting to be excoriated by my wife. Seeing how miserable I was, she pitied me and was sympathetic – reminding me that it was only money and we could make more of it.

We had been burning through money fast, eating at all of New York City's finest Michelin rated restaurants, spending inordinate sums on clothes, a wine collection, and whatever else we felt like buying.

I had presided over a great deal of self-earned wealth for my age and squandered it – like so many other middle class start ups who tried and failed for as long as man and enterprise went hand in hand. I was aware of this distinction and was determined to be exceptional, to forgo the pre-determined path that had been traveled and worn for people like me.

But first I needed to brood and melt away into the comfort that I had made for myself, slowly becoming aware and growing fearful that all of it might be in jeopardy.

Chapter V

"Well, it was a nice try old sport. The Qualcomm should've been left in the well. Then again, losing only 40% on a position isn't all that bad, when compared with my 100% personal loss," I said to Giovanni, dripping with sarcasm.

Gallows humor had not only crept into the office, it ruled it.

"Losing 40% is just as good as up," cried Giovanni. "Heck, George, we should try to get some referrals off this, maybe have the girl send out some letters to our clients -- asking for some names and numbers of their friends and family?"

"That's a splendid idea. You always know what's best," I said. "What should our next pick be – maybe go back to another old well, like Harmonic Lightwaves?"

"God no," Giovanni shrieked. "That fucking thing nearly gave me a stroke. When we had that thing, I thought I was going to die. At least with Qualcomm, I knew we were losing money in a great company. It felt honorable."

"Very true," I declared. "Why don't we ask the coldcallers for a stock pick? Perhaps they're the next Warren Buffetts and we just don't know it because we always task them with pitching our awful picks."

"Another great idea, George," said Giovanni with a great grand smile planted on his cheerful face.

I kicked open the door and yelled out, "any of you bastards know of a good stock we can buy?"

Eric looked at me with his big blue vacant eyes and said "how the fuck should we know? You guys are the experts."

"Did you hear that Giovanni? Eric said we're the experts."

"Yes, we're experts at wiping out accounts. Clients come to us when they need to offset gains with tax losses."

"Hey, we should advertise that in the Times," I said. "Open an account with us, George and Giovanni – the tax loss experts."

"It'll read, 'get the cocksucking IRS off your backs, get FREE TAX LOSSES guaranteed, or your money back,'" said Giovanni.

I then turned my attention back to Eric, who was enjoying our black humor.

"I've got an idea, Eric. Let's call your dad. He's been on Wall Street forever; he'll know what to do, right?"

Eric smiled and said "let's do it. Put it on speakerphone so we can all hear it."

I dialed Harry and placed the call on speakerphone. Eric greeted his father and told him we wanted to ask him a question and that we were all listening in.

We were laughing like giddy schoolgirls in a bathroom gossiping over the latest kiss, when Harry interrupted our ruckus and grimly declared "you're fucked for at least 15 years. Sell everything and buy bonds, boys."

"Oh, come on Harry. Quit being such a Debby Downer," I said. "We've got the internet, the new economy, cell phones, business to business, so many ways to win. Surely this is just another market correction."

Harry doubled down on his bold prediction and with force this time and said, "you're fucked for at least 15 years."

He then explained, "listen, maybe I'm wrong. But I've been on the street for a long time and this is the real deal. Soon you'll start to hear about cash calls and liquidity crunches. All of these fucking companies are bleeding out cash and will go bankrupt because they can't raise money in the equity markets anymore. Without a source of capital, most of them won't be able to survive and will go bankrupt inside of a year. So, if you look at the market from a liquidity standpoint, given the recent losses in stocks, it's only a matter of time before things get really bad. You haven't seen anything yet."

Shortly after that monologue, I thanked him for his input and ended the call.

"Gee what a fucking buzzkill," I said.

Eric said, "don't pay attention to my Dad. He hates all of the dot coms and has been shorting them, hoping they'd collapse."

"Ah ha, that explains it," said Giovanni. "Your Dad is a fucking bearshitter."

"Most definitely," Eric conceded.

"Harry the Bearshitter has declared we are all fucked for at least 15 years. Pack up your things now and head on over to the soup lines for supper," I shouted.

Giovanni laughed and we all had a grand time making fun of old Harry the Bearshitter, the dinosaur of Wall Street who was washed up and didn't know what the hell he was talking about. In spite of our ruinous losses, we sometimes pretended they didn't exist and behaved like we did in December of 1999.

During the summer of 2000, a respite swept the market and traces of a former glory kicked in. The Nasdaq rose 24% and spirits were high again, as most believed the worst had been realized and it was smooth sailing until year end. After all, what craven beast of a man would short stocks heading into the holiday season?

Our business had stabilized too, and we were opening a lot of new accounts, rebuilding and cautiously optimistic. In an odd way, I felt relieved that I wiped out my personal account. It was no longer a burden and I could focus all of my energies into the business. I chalked up my former dreams of trading for a living as an episode in naiveté and an unrealistic delusion brought on through desperation.

Our firm had just announced another acquisition, a Long Island based brokerage firm that specialized in small cap investment banking deals. To commiserate the merger, our firm was hosting a top producers dinner at a quaint downtown restaurant in Little Italy.

It was advertised to us as an 'opportunity to get to know each other' – but we instinctively hated brokers from Long Island and viewed them as reprobates. Giovanni and I marked it on our calendars and went about our day enjoying the sweet violent melodies of rap music, which was turned up to riotous levels at night.

Our former grandeur was creeping through the purple gloom, broken by laughter and an increase in production.

While at times infuriating, being a broker was incredibly rewarding when times were good and we all strived for that calm normality, like a drug losing its potency.

One late afternoon, I grabbed Chuck to get a quick bite. As we were walking through the boardroom, we spotted a familiar face.

"Is that who I think it is?", I said.

Chuck shouted out across the nearly vacated boardroom, "holy shit, is that you Frank?"

Frank was a portly man with a giant round face, roughly 35 years old. His warm eyes jumped around a lot and he had a nervous twitch in his long nose, which made him constantly rub it.

Gently, he replied, "hey Chuck, how is everything?"

I introduced myself and said "hi, I'm George. You probably don't remember me at the old firm. I was just starting out and wasn't even licensed at the time; but I was a big fan of your salesmanship."

"Thank you, George," said Frank. "That's very kind of you."

Chuck was thrilled to see Frank working at our firm and I could see the excitement beaming from his face.

"So, when did you get here? What are you pitching?", asked Chuck.

"Oh, I got here about a month ago. I'm not pitching anything now, just getting leads."

"Here a month and you haven't turned his boardroom into a riot? What the fuck happened to you?"

"No, not yet," said Frank with a half-hearted laugh.

"Well, it was good seeing you Frank. We'll catch up later."

"You too Chuck. Hey, nice to meet you George."

Frank was a legend at the first firm I ever worked for, known for being an absolute killer on the phones, able to close sales almost at will – and now he appeared to be broken, a shadow of the person he used to be. This made both Chuck and I melancholy, seeing a great man reduced to quietly cold calling stale leads in a desolate boardroom, filled with inferiors.

Based solely on discipline and professionality, the firm I knew Frank from was the best firm I ever worked for. The sales force was extremely proud and efficient, morale was high, and the atmosphere was electric. It's hard to describe it with words; only those who were able to experience it and see it with their own eyes understood that true greatness had resided in that place, located in midtown Manhattan, circa 1997, before it all went wrong.

The boardroom was enormous and wide open like an airplane hangar. The decor was reserved -- dark rugs, glass offices without blinds, and a sea of gray desks that connected to one another. The top producers sat right next to the pikers – which generated a vibrant atmosphere of talent and work ethic spreading throughout the boardroom like an infectious virus.

Brokers weren't allowed to have stock quotes on their computers – because it was a distraction. The mailroom was fitted with a lead store, where brokers could purchase leads from the firm. They were the best leads I've ever called, because they were the best leads money could buy.

The boardroom was never quiet. Brokers were on their feet, pitching all day long, with some of the hungrier ones staying through the night to call California, and the hungriest amongst them would stay even later to call Hawaii.

As a coldcaller, I was expected to get 10 leads per day for my mentor, who was the biggest producer at the firm.

Scott was a studious looking man, with a slender build, and thinned framed spectacles – impeccably dressed. He was the most talented salesman I've ever known and his confidence radiated around him. We all strived to be like Scott, and not just because he was successful, but because he was truly an inspirational figure. He'd often visit me at night, in the back of the boardroom where the coldcaller pits were situated, as I was trying hard to get my 10th lead, which was a standard of excellence amongst coldcallers.

He'd show me his new $80,000 watches, or diamond cufflinks, and talk about his new Ferrari, and how grand his life was. He didn't do this to brag or make me feel awful about my impoverished existence, but to motivate me to want more.

Frank wasn't in the top ranks of producers at the firm – but he had gusto and was up and coming. He outworked everyone, wilding pacing up and down the aisle adjacent to his desk -- pouring his heart and soul out on the phone to prospective clients. He developed a reputation for being an amazing account opener, which was more of a byproduct of talent and not work ethic. When he wasn't pitching new accounts, Frank could be seen walking around the firm with a notepad and a pen, taking notes of the sales pitches that appealed to him. He was a storehouse for good raps.

Our leader, the owner of the firm, was a tall dapper 30-something man named Charles. He had pale skin, dark brown eyes, and heavily gelled brown hair slicked back. He rarely joked and was always focused on business, or trying to motivate his salesforce to do better. In the few times I spoke to him, he was kind and gave me the impression that he cared about his employees, always offering me sound advice and encouragement.

All of my fellow coldcallers in the pit idolized Charles and spoke of him as being the epitome of success, the quintessential combination of great genes and breeding.

Charles would preside over legendary morning and afternoon meetings, where he'd take to the microphone to address his army of brokers. They were always unique monologues, filled with great advice, especially for youngsters starting out.

At one morning meeting, I remember him asking us, "do you know the difference between you and me?", quietly surveying the room with poise and in complete control, waiting for the perfect opportunity to reveal his answer. He could've said "I'm a space alien magician" and we would've nodded and believed him.

"The answer is time," Charles said. "If I lost my entire book of business today, I could rebuild a brand new one inside of one year and match my production numbers. I am not the result of my book of clients, they are the manifestation of me."

We ate it up and begged for more.

During one of Charles' epic morning speeches, a top producer came strutting in 10 minutes late, which was an unacceptable offense at the firm. Whenever I was late, I'd hide in the bathroom with the others, hoping to sneak in undetected after the meeting had ended.

"What the fuck are you doing?", Charles said to the top producer walking in late. "You're supposed to be here at 8am, no exceptions. $1,000 fine."

"But, Charles, the train was late. What the fuck?"

"I don't give a shit, $1,000 fine. Speak again and it'll be $10,000," said Charles with an expressionless countenance.

Frank had catapulted to celebrity status at the firm during one of Charles' morning meetings. Before the meetings began, everyone hung up their phones and sat in their chairs, eagerly awaiting oratory splendor. But on this one rare occasion, someone had continued to pitch. Upon hearing the chatter, Charles stepped down from his podium to investigate who'd dare interrupt his meeting. It was Frank. Much to my surprise, Charles seized up when he approached Frank, seeing how animated he was – pacing up and down the aisle – trying his best to convince the person on the other end of the phone to buy. He stood there for a moment and marveled at Frank's passion -- and then he upped the ante and piped the call into the firm's audio system that projected out to more than 10 speakers around the firm, all in Dolby stereo.

Now it was a show, with a captive audience of 200 listening into every syllable coming out of Frank's energetic mouth.

"Frank, I told you, now's not a good time," said the prospect named Phil. "I will watch the stock and would love to hear from you in the future, but I got to go. I can't do this now."

"Hang on a second," Frank interjected emphatically. "I can certainly appreciate that Phil, but here's what I propose we do instead. You and I both know that you're never gonna watch the stock, no one does that. In all honesty, I'm only calling you and being so persistent because I know this stock is going higher" – with an emphasis on 'know' – "and I understand how lasting relations are built – through trusting someone and coming through for them during times of uncertainty. That's the foundation I'm looking to start with you today."

"Why don't we do this?" he continued. "If you want to play the stock, pick up a block of 100,000 shares and I'll fly you out to New York for steaks and cigars when we sell it for a huge profit. But since you just want to watch it and judge me on this one trade, say no to me and buy 100 shares, and watch it through your monthly account statements. I know it might seem like a waste of time, but trust me, it'll be worth it in the end, not only for this stock – but for gaining access to my network and connections on Wall Street. I'll title the account individually and have my secretary discuss the details with you; but, please Phil, make a commitment to me that when this stock does exactly what I said it's gonna do, you'll never embarrass me again and make me work this hard for such a small order and you'll wire in some real money to fund the account. Fair enough?"

Then there was an awkward silence for a solid 10 seconds, but it felt like an eternity. Everyone knew to shut up after asking for an order to buy – scared to blow it by talking too much.

As we waited for Phil to answer, Frank turned to his audience, his face red and radiating with virility. With one hand, he held a shiny black phone to his ear, the other was a palm waiving in the air to us, as if to say 'shhh, not a fucking word you bastards, just wait for it.'

Phil broke, "Ok Frank, let's do it."

Frank said, "thank you for the vote of confidence," then he transferred the call to his assistant -- and then he fist pumped into the air.

And the crowd went fucking apeshit.

The second that call ended, I knew I'd remember it for the rest of my life. My good friend sitting next to me, Gene, who was a terrific salesman and very manly, was crying with joy after bearing witness to that sale.

Frank stepped up to the plate when it counted most and closed the deal. But now, just a few years later, mired in a disgusting market collapse, Frank wasn't the same animated man filled with verve, but instead a solemn ghost of his former self -- sitting at the ass-end of the boardroom right outside Dave's office fetching leads.

Chapter VI

On Wednesday, September 27th 2000, the top producers at our New York City office went downtown to break bread with the newest members of the firm – a cadre of gauche savages clad in pinstripe suits drenched in musky cologne, hailing from Long Island.

Most of them wore bold colors, were very tan, and spoke like they were from Brooklyn, circa 1955. There was a certain wildness to these people. They had shifty eyes, short tempers, and were hyper-aggressive – all of the qualities needed to be a successful stockbroker.

The venue was located in a small restaurant in Little Italy. When I walked in, I felt like I was stepping back in time, an easier era when men ate grotesquely large bowls of linguini, a loaf of bread, and two bottles of Chianti for supper every night. There were a dozen round tables adorned with red and white table cloths, each having a single small candle in its center. The walls were festooned with dark framed photographs of celebrities in joyous scenes at the restaurant, harking back to the glory days of this haunt -- amongst them was Frank Sinatra and Dean Martin, naturally.

In the back was a small bar, bedecked with rich mahogany – manned by a balding bartender with a thick mustache, probably 55 years of age. Most of the waiters were Italian and Giovanni made quick friends with several of them, addressing them in their native tongue.

They were all very professional, almost stoic, moving quickly throughout the dining room filling glasses with fresh water and placing large baskets of warm bread onto each table.

Just like the previous top producers meeting, I was seated next to the firm's top producer, Steve – a man in a perpetual state of anger, always in need to vent about some grave injustice the firm had levied upon him.

"Look at these cocksuckers," said Steve – "they look like extras from a Martin Scorsese film. I can't believe we bought these absolute clowns."

Giovanni chimed in, "hey Steve, how are you guys doing? Have you been managing the market okay?"

"Not bad. I lost like $5 million in Cisco, other than that – fucking great. You guys holding clients in or getting hit with ACATs?"

"Luckily, we only lost a few," I said. "I think our clients are too shocked to fire us just yet. They'll probably get around to it by the end of the year."

Steve nodded his head in agreement and said "that's when they'll do it. Those cocksuckers always fire you at the end of the year. Rich people are very ritualistic about New Year's. We're all gonna get fucked by Christmas."

By 7:30pm, the room was filled with a sea of strange faces, all glaring at us with jaundiced expressions. Steve was sitting back drinking copious amounts of red wine, sizing up every single

unfamiliar face with his beady black eyes. Across from him sat Nick, joyous as ever – chain smoking and making small talk with some of the new faces, some of which were decidedly less jaundiced.

Our sales manager, Mike, stood up and held an empty wine glass in the air and hit it repeatedly with a spoon to gain our undivided attention.

"Thank you for coming," declared Mike. "As many of you know, our parent company made another acquisition and I'd like to make a few announcements, as well as give you some news. I'm happy to announce, starting January 2nd, 2001, we're moving to a new office in the famed Chrysler Building in New York City. We will keep an office open in Long Island, but encourage all to move to NYC to fill up the office. It's a fantastic space, completely renovated. Everything is brand new. It will be the flagship office for our American operations."

Everyone gave a sympathetic round of applause.

"In addition to that, I'd like to introduce the CEO of our newly acquired firm from Long Island, who will be serving with me as Executive Vice President, in charge of investment banking operations in America. Rudolph, come up here and say a word or two."

Although we loved Mike because he was one of us, he had a slimy way about him, like a snake slithering through the tall grass. Next to Rudolph, Mike looked like an ordinary thief, outclassed and diminutive in both stature and presence.

The Long Island brokers gave a rowdy round of applause for Rudolph, accompanied by some hollering and whistling. This instantly irritated Steve, who looked like he was about to flip the table over and start breaking bottles over their heads.

I instantly liked Rudolph; we all did, except Steve. He had kind eyes, in his mid 50s, was tall, and had a dark Italian complexion like my Grandfather's in late summer after weeks of bathing in the blistering Brooklyn sun. Unlike Mike, who was an attorney and never ran a book, Rudolph had street cred as a deal maker, a boss who fought with his troops in the trenches, with a long track record of success. I knew why the Long Island brokers liked him – Rudolph was a man's man and I was pleased to have him jointly leading our firm with Mike.

Rudolph stood up and calmly waited for everyone to settle down and give him their attention.

"Ladies and gentlemen, thank you for attending this meeting. I am honored to join this great firm and look forward to working with many of you in the future. Looking out into this room, we have some sharp looking men and ladies here tonight and I am excited to get to know each and every one of you. I'm not going to take up your time with a long speech, but just know that my door is always open to any of you, for any reason." He then raised a glass filled with white wine and said "salud."

"Look at this fucking greaseball," said Steve with a ravenous look in his eyes. "Where's his fucking Tommy Gun? It's fitting we're in Little Italy now; we're probably all gonna get wacked by these cocksuckers by the end of the night."

Giovanni shot back, "relax Steve, you fucking lunatic." He raised a glass and said "cheers."

Steve acquiesced: "cheers to you too, Giovanni."

After dinner, sensing a possible shift in power at the firm, Giovanni made a beeline for Rudolph and made small talk. They seemed to hit it off great, speaking Italian to one another --- patting each other on the back, sharing healthy laughs. Steve and I joined Nick at the bar, who was engaged in what looked like an amicable conversation with several of the Long Island brokers.

I was introduced to Sean, Milton, and Glenn. Apparently, Glenn was the largest producer at the Long Island firm – a tall man, maybe 6'3", with a 5 O'clock shadow, and shaggy brown hair. I instantly hated him. He looked bitter and resentful.

"So, what are you guys buying?", asked Glenn with involuntary smugness.

Steve instinctively answered, "what difference does it make? The fucking market is a zoo. I lost $7 million in Cisco since March."

Glenn laughed and then swallowed the balance of his glass of scotch.

Nick was the life of the party, hamming it up at the bar, and it seemed to annoy Glenn – who grimaced at Nick while engorging himself in another glass of scotch.

"Are you gay or something?", asked Glenn – touching Nick on his shoulder.

"Hey buddy," said Nick. "You ok? I think you might've had a little too much to drink."

"Don't change the argument, pal. I asked you a question," pressed Glenn with increasing condescension.

"What do you want? How can I make you go away?" said Nick, flustered by Glenn's rudeness.

"Are you a faggot?", insisted Glenn.

"No, but I get that a lot, um-kay," replied Nick with an awkward laugh. "Now get lost," flippantly dismissing Glenn with a hand gesture.

Seeing this unfold, Steve put down his glass of red wine and got in Glenn's face and challenged, "what difference is it to you, you fucking cocksucker?"

Steve had become unmoored.

He continued in the most animated of fashions, "If my friend Nick wants to choke on a fucking barrel of dicks, it's none of your fucking business. Ok? That's the problem with you Long Island cocksuckers, you're all a bunch of animals. Do us all a favor pal and go back to the woods where you belong and fuck your field goats."

He then pointed to Sean and Milton and stated plainly, "and take these fucking clowns with you too."

Glenn lunged and threw a roundhouse swing at Steve, but missed.

Rudolph ran over and broke up the melee, grabbing Glenn by the shoulder. Steve shouted a few profanities and was pulled to the side by Mike.

The tension in the room became untenable, a lurid showdown between the NYC slicksters and Long Island cocksuckers loomed large. All of the Long Island brokers rallied to the side of Glenn, conspiring with him, offering him support while shooting daggers at us. In turn, we gathered around Steve, our unelected leader, and waited for resolution. At any moment, I felt Tommy Guns would be brandished, reducing the whole place to Swiss cheese.

"Fellas, we all had a lot of drink. Let's call it a night and put this ugliness behind us," begged Rudolph. "We're all professionals here. Please, let's act like it," attempting to part the crowd and alleviate the strain.

Rudolph was now commanding a presence in the room.

"Glenn come here." He then pointed to Steve and said, "I'm sorry, what's your name?"

"My name is Steve and you should tell your animal over there (pointing to Glenn) that if he tries to lay his hands on me again, I'll break his fucking jaw for him."

Glenn stood in the center of the room next to Rudolph, with a hard boiled face, sloshing around a bit from the effects of the liquor.

With a calming cadence, Rudolph said, "boys, let's shake hands and call it a night. Come on, do it for me." He grabbed Glenn and Steve by the shoulders and insisted, "shake hands fellas. Put this silliness behind us. We're all professionals here."

The two men shook hands and the tension broke. There was a lot of idle chatter and irreverent laughter happening in the background. But the violent energy was mostly gone from the room and people began to slowly dawdle out of the restaurant, spilling out into the cool New York City streets.

"What a shit-show," I said to Nick.

"Tell me about it. Hey, do you and Giovanni want to head back to midtown to get a few?", asked Nick

Giovanni said, "sure. Hey, we should invite Glenn too. What do ya say?", laughing maniacally.

I thought he was kidding, but Giovanni went straight over to pixilated Glenn and said, "hey Glenn, Giovanni here." They shook hands. "Me and my buddy George and Nick are gonna head back up to midtown for a few drinks. Want to join us and bury the hatchet?"

Glenn quickly declined Giovanni's friendly offer with a "no thanks" and trailed behind us as we made our way out of the restaurant. While stepping down the short flight of steps leading out to the streets, Glenn tapped on Nick's shoulder and said, "so, are you a fucking fag?"

Without hesitation, Nick whirled around and laid him out cold, dropping all 75 inches of Glenn to the gray pavement. An eerie silence immediately followed, as Glenn's friends sheepishly helped him off the ground.

The top producers dinner had finally ended, notwithstanding a grand finale that was sure to be talked about amidst the gossipers at the water cooler the next day.

We then got into a cab and headed back to midtown for a nightcap, regaling Nick as our hero in our triumphant and glorious victory against the 'Long Island cocksuckers.' He didn't pay for a drink for the remainder of the night.

The next day, Nick was fined $1,000 to be donated to Glenn's charity of choice.

Chapter VII

The merriment that had radiated throughout our office that summer had spoiled in the autumn and rotted during the winter. The immensities of the drawdowns took a toll on the firm and people started to quit, to find work that paid a livable wage. The skeletal remains of the boardrooms took on a garish and foreboding journey into fear. The gallows were very crowded with well dressed men clad in three piece Armani suits and Bruno Magli shoes. There were two schools of men in the final days of 2000, the ones who skipped across the dead sea like smooth pebbles, carving out rivulets of income from a sinister and rakish market, the other being the maudlin, parasitic faineantise – idlers who drowned in their pity.

Mike butchered a good 20% of the workforce before moving into our new pristine headquarters in the famed Chrysler Building – an art deco skyscraper that was built during the Great Depression. Our business was plodding along no worse than all of the other top producers – steadily, but assuredly, losing volume, only sustained by new accounts and the fortunate strike of luck. The Nasdaq bled heavily into Christmas and the New Year's – mostly because the dithering Federal Reserve seized up and watched us all burn. They hiked rates all the way up to 6.5%, fearing an overheating economy, even hiking in May – and did nothing but watch as the market got slaughtered and the economy began to crumble, for the balance of the year. Wall Street wanted an interest rate cut and they wanted it badly. They needed it, after dissipating away all year – racked for 50% from the Nasdaq's March 10th highs.

After the New Year's, what was left of our firm limped into the gilded offices of the Chrysler Building, accompanied by our new friends from Long Island. Much to my surprise, Giovanni and I weren't given an office – but the very next thing – a small area in the front boardroom, brightly lit, with ample space to seat our staff.

It was a grand space, replete with endless desks and computers -- walls bursting with gray, lined with glass offices, accompanied by standard corporate grade charcoal Berber carpet. Our new sales manager was a former analyst, who once shared a wall with us back in the old office and was regularly tortured by Giovanni and his late night rap music sessions.

Chase was about 5'11", slender build, artificially tanned, and immaculately dressed. Giovanni used to say, "I bet that guy is tanning his ass in the office, while we're out here in this bastard boardroom dialing for dollars." He was rather sore about being kicked into the boardroom; but I didn't mind it one bit and welcomed the change of scenery, getting to know new people who had an interest in hard work and building a business.

Chase always wore his blazer, adorned with a portico styled pocket square, confidently moving throughout the firm without a single hair on his head out of place. In the early days of 2001, he was the firm's executioner, culling the workforce in order to redistribute dead books of business. Most brokers held onto their legacy dot com positions, all dreadfully down, unable to realize what was already known; the party had ended and we were in the depths of a terrible bear market. By firing brokers and giving their clients to top producers, the firm was able to close out losing trades, generate commissions, and hopefully convert dormant clients into active ones. I had a fairly good relationship with Chase, since he and I shared similar vanities, and I used this relationship to get on the short list of receiving the accounts from brokers recently fired, also called 'inherited accounts.'

On Wednesday, January 3rd 2001, our second day in the new office, the Fed slashed interest rates by 25 basis points, producing a surreal spike in stocks. The Nasdaq catapulted higher by 14%, and just about everyone in the office was overwhelmed with pure joy. Over the next two days, however, things reverted back to the mean and the Nasdaq shed 8%, and Chase fired 5 brokers -- which became a Friday ritual at the new firm. If you weren't doing at least $10,000 in monthly gross commissions, you were most definitely being looked at by Chase. That beautiful new office, teeming with promise and vim, had a dark side to it and was soon to be known as the killing fields for low producing brokers.

I immersed myself in the new corporate culture that washed through the firm. I attended all the meetings and took copious notes and considered myself to be a team player. The old George had been killed in the tragic drama of 2000, along with all of his stocks, and a new one emerged in 2001, one focused on self-improvement. I groomed myself and began to absorb information on an industrial scale, from classic literature, epicurean delights, to learning about true leadership in business; I wanted to learn all I could because I felt that by becoming better, I could attract a higher echelon clientele. My demeanor changed too, bordering on staid priggishness, almost a 180 degree reversal from my former gun slinging days of margin calls, drunken cold calls, and internet stocks bursting out and busting down.

Giovanni resented all of the change, and although he was more than able to communicate in the language that Chase chose to speak, he opted against it and considered the corporate culture to be a cancer. He wasn't the only one.

Steve was situated in a gigantic office just around the corner from us, right next to Chase's. One afternoon in late January, he came to pay us a visit. Since the firm was rapidly sacking all of the old familiar faces, Steve latched onto us and made us his best friends at the firm, or at least someone he could complain to – which was his favorite thing to do.

"Fellas, come into my office for a minute. I want to ask you question," Steve demanded, visibly angered by something.

Giovanni and I went into his office and sat across from his desk and he began.

"Can I ask you a question? How many inherited accounts did you get this week?"

I said, "I don't know, maybe 50 or 60."

"Really?", said Steve. "Not for nothing fellas, but I'm doing a hell of a lot more production than you now and should be getting more. Look at this shit," showing us a printout of inherited accounts he just received from Chase after the last round of firings. "I barely got 100."

Giovanni laughed at Steve's ridiculous plight, chalking it up to some sort of dead pan humor. "Come on, Steve. These are free accounts – just be grateful to get something, you jerkoff."

"Grateful, grateful?", said Steve in a highly animated tone. "Let me tell you something (practically foaming at the mouth), I've done $10 million gross for these cocksuckers over the past three years. I expect to get more than a lousy $3 million in inherited accounts, when there's probably $30 million out there. Who knows how much these bastards are keeping for themselves? They better step up and give me more. It's time for them to wash my back, know what I mean? Fucking wash my back."

"Indeed, they should wash your back," I said.

Steve nodded in agreement, glad that someone understood his deleterious position.

Giovanni and I realized there was no reasoning with Steve. He wanted the firm to fire more brokers so that he could take their clients – because he deserved it and needed his back washed.

One afternoon, after receiving "just $8 million in new assets" from Chase, an enraged Steve stormed into Mike's office and got himself fired. From what I was able to gather, Steve screamed at Mike for 5 minutes straight about 'being fucked' by the firm and berated Mike by calling him 'a cocksucker' three or four times, before Mike had enough of Steve and asked for his resignation. After Steve left the firm, he started his own firm and tried to recruit us by offering us a 100% payout on our commissions for 6 months. We respectfully declined his most generous offer, but wished him well.

In an ironic twist of fate, we inherited many of Steve's accounts – most of whom hated his guts and opted to stay with us rather than leave with him.

In early February 2000, my coldcaller Eric got a new account from someone he met at a Christmas party.

I remember the moment he told me about the account; it was his largest new account to date. He was very excited and proud. Eric wasn't a very effective broker and had a tendency to loaf around a lot, often leaving early and taking unexplained days off from work, rather than work hard. He was like that as a child too, always taking short cuts in school, or placing little effort in sports, which in the end hurt him. I often reminded him that if he hadn't grow up with me in the same apartment building, I'd fire him 10 ways till Sunday.

"I got this guy to invest $100k," Eric said with an expression of bliss. "He could be a whale. He said he owns about 6 taxi medallions and is probably worth millions."

Happy to see him make some progress, I said "that's really great Eric. Well done, let's –"

Giovanni interrupted, "let's see what this guy is about," quickly grabbing the account paperwork, reviewing the numbers. He called Vlad and welcomed him aboard 'our team' and then quickly made a series of recommendations – all fairly aggressive tech stocks, which were all accepted by Vlad, who told Giovanni he wanted to 'make a lot of money' in the fastest way possible – to recoup some of the losses he endured during the dot com crash. Vlad was a Russian immigrant and had a thick accent. He promised to send us 'a lot more money' if we performed well with the initial $100,000.

Vlad's investments performed miserably right from the start, tracking the Nasdaq in lock step lower – which had dropped by 30% over the next two months. The losses hit Vlad hard and caused him to call us up 5-10 times per day, panicking about his investments. We treated his account like anyone else's and tried to explain to him that although his account was lower – it was tracking the broader indices and would recover once the market rebounded. But for some reason, he thought we were in control of the market and would beg us to 'do something' to make his stocks trade higher.

One afternoon, he came to visit us to have lunch, wanting to discuss his account. He was sloppily dressed in a black jumpsuit, ornamented with grease stains from maybe a pork chop he had just been eating. We took him to the Bryant Park Café and were seated outdoors. It was early April and the weather was warm and the faint signs of spring were abundant, with dozens of other well dressed New Yorkers cavorting in the elegant small park in front of us.

Giovanni was annoyed by Vlad. I knew this because of his body language. He barely made eye contact with him and began to squirm around in his chair, as if he was dying to excuse himself to the bathroom. After 5 minutes of idle chatter, Giovanni snapped and yelled out to our waiter, who was maybe 30 feet away from us, "young man, please come here."

"Yes, Sir, how might I help you?," asked the waiter.

"Look at this water. Don't you see it?", scolded Giovanni.

The waiter inquisitively examined the glass of perfectly normal water in Giovanni's hands and then sheepishly looked into Giovanni's bulging blue eyes and gave a shrug with his shoulders.

Giovanni continued, "It's pink and disgusting." He then took the contents of the thick crystal glass and threw it onto the ground, declaring "now get me some clean water that isn't pink."

Shocked by the tantrum, the waiter quickly took the glass and brought it directly to the head waiter and then pointed at us.

"Great job psycho," I whispered. "Now you're gonna get us kicked out of here with crazy fucking Vlad with us."

Vlad was as quiet as a mouse, timidly observing the events transpiring in front of him, most likely amazed at Giovanni's violent reaction to being served pink water.

The head waiter came over to our table, but before he could say a word, Giovanni said "you guys should be ashamed of yourselves, serving us filthy water like that. I know the owner of this place and will see to it that he is made aware."

Giovanni didn't know the owner, but said it anyway, in the hopes it would sway the head waiter from tossing us out.

"I am very sorry, Sir," said the head waiter – who was sincerely apologetic for having served Giovanni a glass of pink water. "Your waiter will provide you with some sparkling water, on the house of course. Again, we're very sorry for the inconvenience."

I made sure to avoid eating anything that was served during lunch, fearing the kitchen's wrath on our food. Our client was rambling on about his portfolio, completely ignorant to the events unfolding in the market. He only wished we'd stop clowning around with losing stocks and begin making him back the $300,000 or so he had lost during the bust.

"You guys, come on. I know you can do something, right?", said an anxious Vlad, offering me a candid wink as if to communicate he knew that we could make him money if we really wanted to.

I was revolted by the suggestion, especially since these alleged powers that I was being accused of having did me no good just a year prior, when I wiped out my entire brokerage account.

"Vlad, the Nasdaq is down 30% over the same time period you've been invested with us," I said. "Your account is down roughly 26%, which means you're outperforming. Just hang in there and wait for the market to bounce. We don't have control over these things, you know."

The phrase 'just hang in there' was our favorite line to clients back then. In retrospect, it was a double entendre.

Vlad nodded his head and repeated his desire to 'make a little bit of money' and hoped we'd change our mind about 'making his account go higher.'

A week after our lunch meeting, Vlad called Tom, who was our newly appointed manager, to complain about his investments, which led to the account being frozen and stripped away from our management.

Tom was a middle aged man with thick eyeglasses and an out-of-date mustache. He was a large man, but not tall, and he was severely austere in almost every way, from his manner of clothing to his investments. Against this background, every once in a while, he would blurt out the most vile profanities due to his feverish involvement in politics – which always shocked us and made us question his sanity. One of his most hated political figures of all time was FDR, who Tom said 'was a fucking bastard cocksucking communist.' Politics aside, Tom was as righteous and just as a church mouse.

Tom sat right in back of us and I could tell that he initially hated our guts, most likely because we cold called for new clients all day long. Tom got clients the old fashioned way, through nepotism and family money.

He once accused me of "cramming stock down the throats of old ladies," which enraged me and caused me to shame him for a solid two hours about the virtues of hard work and how I hadn't ever 'crammed stock' down anyone's throat. I read Tom perfectly and knew exactly what he wanted to hear and it wasn't long before we became good friends.

Vlad began to pester Tom during the day, calling him once per hour about his investments – begging him to insert profits into his beleaguered account. These suggestions made Tom recoil and he'd angrily set Vlad in his place and then quickly end the call. This occurred for two weeks, until Vlad made the grave error of asking Tom to trade mutual funds for him, hoping to get in at a discounted NAV during an up day in the market. This caused Tom to lose his mind and close out the account all together. Inside of a month, Vlad filed a complaint with the firm, accusing us of all sorts of crimes, such as churning, fraud, and a laundry list of items his attorney cobbled together.

The charges were completely preposterous and Tom knew it. But our Chief Compliance Officer, a very starched old man name Stan, viewed the charge severely and used it to scold us.

One afternoon in early May, Chase walked over to our work area, accompanied by a grim looking Stan, and asked if Giovanni, Eric, Tom and I would meet them in the conference room to discuss Vlad's complaint. As soon as we entered the room, Stan turned to us and said "you guys are completely screwed. Do you see what you guys did?"

Shocked and taken aback, Giovanni did what Giovanni did best, aggressively lash out, and said "what the fuck are you talking about Stan? We didn't do a damn thing. This client is out of his fucking mind, right Tom?"

Tom agreed and spoke candidly in his heavy midwestern accent, "I have to agree with Giovanni here Stan. Listen, I had been dealing with this client for a good two weeks and he's certainly a character. I got to tell ya, I think he's fucking nuts."

Stan glared at Tom with a knitted brow, as Tom continued "I reviewed the account and the boys did nothing out of the ordinary, other than ride the market down, which is unfortunate, but beyond their control."

Stan saw it differently and said, "I just spoke to the poor guy and he's a taxi driver with no money and you guys messed around with his life's savings with your crazy stock picks. Why, you ought to be ashamed of yourselves."

Eric, who looked like he wanted to soil his pants, chimed in and said, "that isn't true, Sir. I opened this account and he's worth millions. He's not just a taxi driver, but he also owns 6 medallions, which are worth at least $300,000 a piece."

"He doesn't own any medallions," said Stan, angered by Eric's interruption. "Plus, the account statement said his net worth was only $1 million."

Eric started, "well, that's what he asked me to put, but I assumed it was much more than that, Sir. I believe Vlad was being modest when he said that."

Disgusted by Eric's statement, Stan snapped, "it's all the damn same thing anyway, son. You shouldn't have been trading this man's account."

At that point Chase broke the tension and declared we should all simmer down and wait for more facts to come in before rushing to judgement.

"We'll have our attorneys look into this and will be getting back to you," cried Chase. Opening the door for us to leave, he said "gentlemen" – and we left.

"Can you believe this shit, Giovanni?", I said. "We barely even traded the damn account and compliance is shitting their pants over one lousy complaint."

"They don't give a damn about us George," raged Giovanni. "All they want to do is settle these cases, wack the broker, and be done with it."

"But won't it cost more to fight in court than to just settle the case?" I asked.

"We're not settling shit," said Giovanni. "I'd rather die before we settle anything with that jerkoff Vlad."

About a year later, the firm's attorneys coerced us into settling the case by offering to absorb the total cost of the settlement, which was $20,000.

Chapter VIII

On my 25th birthday, exactly one year after I wiped out my entire brokerage account, tensions were high at home. Jackie and I would argue over money, mostly due to me feeling a sense of panic as our savings slipped away. Still burning through $15,000 per month in capricious spending, our savings had dwindled down to $60,000. While things at work were somewhat stable, my production numbers of $30,000 per month wasn't even close to covering my expenses. Slowly but surely, I was heading towards the poorhouse – just where I had started.

Our arguments were loud and impassioned, often leading to joint declarations of breaking up, which rarely lasted more than a few hours. All of our friends seemed to have easier lives, less expenses, more helpful parents, and we took it out on each other – because life wasn't the fairy tale we had imagined. Young and beautiful, we were supposed to be sharing cocktails by the beach at 25, care free, listening to our favorite music. Instead, I worked from 8am to 9pm every night but Friday, and she was catering to every whim of our son, keeping a clean house, making sure I had something to eat when I got home.

"I don't know what else to do, Jackie. No matter how hard I work, no matter how much effort I put into this damned business, it's just not enough."

What she said to me next stood with me for years and I always remembered it when things got hard.

"This is our journey and we shouldn't be fearful of it. Every story has its arc and this is ours. All of the hard work you're putting in now will pay off later. You've always been able to get us out of a mess and you've done incredible things the past few years."

On the weekends, we'd take George to play at the park. There was this one place near the water with a view of the Verrazano bridge. It was an aspirational view, the type of view that you saw and said to yourself 'one day I will live in a house with a view like this.' The park wasn't very large, but big enough for us. The salt water breeze swept through the green fields and brought the sweet smells of vanilla grass and honeysuckle to our sun kissed faces. The fields were littered with yellow dandelions, some of them puffy and white. We'd teach George that those were the ones you'd pick to blow on and make a wish. Sometimes we'd fly kites and I'd run for hours trying to get the darn thing to stay up in the air. Afterwards, we'd head over to a family owned Italian restaurant to wash up and eat something hearty and warm. More often than not, George would reject anything but chicken nuggets and French fries; but every once in a while, I got him to eat something new and I cherished those moments because I felt it was making him a better person.

Jackie and I talked about having more children, but I could barely afford the three of us and I didn't want to bring another person into the world while times were hard. Nevertheless, we felt that it was our duty, whether we liked it or not, to provide George with a sibling – because one day we'd be gone and we didn't want him to be alone. We agreed to revisit the conversation in a year. Jackie promised me that work would get better and we'd have enough money to do whatever we wanted.

It was an admirable trait of hers, being optimistic like that. Throughout my entire life, I've only known hardship and struggle, so it wasn't easy for me to simply relax and let the chips fall in my lap. I had to work for it and if it felt easy, it wasn't real or enough.

I intensified my efforts at work and truly worked with Dean and Eric to land some accounts. I came up with the idea to start targeting big accounting firm employees and it ended up being a great idea. By the end of the summer in 2001, markets were on a tear again, higher by 23% since June 1st and we were gathering some significant clients and assets.

Chase continued to fire 5 brokers each and every Friday and the firm started to move away from retail stockbrokers like us. They hired a group of 10 institutional brokers and seated them directly in front of us. They all looked very happy and comfortable, unaffected by the bear market. Giovanni resented them more than anyone else at the firm – because they'd just sit there and do nothing all day, pick up the phone, and drop $20 million trades.

"I'm still waiting for my phone to ring and for someone to tell me to buy them 500,000 shares of IBM," Giovanni said to me during an early September rant.

Truth was, most of the institutional brokers did nothing but gossip all day, waiting around for one of their gigantic clients to call, then do $20,000 in commissions for the day. To us, they had the best jobs in the world and it made our plight seem all the more futile.

We knew exactly what everyone was doing at the firm because Chuck had been given administrative access to the trading terminal, by accident of course. Chuck had God-like powers to see everyone's assets under management, production, and trades -- and he used this information to his advantage on numerous occasions, especially when striking up casual discussions with other brokers at the firm. It was incredibly creepy, but we, admittedly, appreciated the tidbits of information he imparted to us.

Chuck was struggling with his production numbers, barely escaping Chase's bloody hatchet – probably because he spent most of his time spying on everyone else.

I read a lot back then, mostly classics by Tolstoy, Dickens, Fitzgerald, and Hemingway. I figured I could get to the new stuff later, after I caught up with the great literature that had been written over the past 200 years. My commute was about an hour each way; and in the mornings, I took an express bus, which cost me $4. It was a luxury expense, but I truly hated the subways.

One morning in early September, I slumbered out of bed late and boarded the express bus in Bay Ridge Brooklyn en route for midtown Manhattan, armed with Tolstoy's War and Peace. Prince Andrei was leading the charge against the Napoleonic invaders, fighting bravely and with honor. It was a wonderful day and I remember gazing into the blue skies and thinking about how perfect it looked, like an endless blue canvas enveloping the brightest sun I've ever seen. The bus stopped at the Millennium Hotel, NYC at 8:45 am and about 20 people filed out of the bus and streamed onto the pavement, crossing over and walking towards the World Trade Center. I was ensconced in Tolstoy's world, amazed by how beautifully he wrote. The French army, led by Napoleon, was quickly advancing towards Moscow, and the Russian aristocrats were entangled in societal upheaval – struggling to adjust to the harsh realities of war and what it bore.

As the bus began to move through the heavily trafficked area, a gigantic explosion rattled the earth. It sounded like 10 car explosions at once and no one knew where the sound came from. Suddenly, our bus was showered with thousands of little pieces of paper. It reminded me of the recent ticket tape parades that rained down on the triumphant NY Yankees, but in an overtly ominous way.

Then someone looked up and pointed towards a gaping hole in one of the towers that had flames bursting out of it -- and the women on the bus began to howl, tears streaming down their faces as they watched in horror; an unmistakable tragedy was unfolding right in front of us. Immediately I thought of the stories my Grandfather told me about a time long ago when a small airplane accidentally crashed into the Empire State Building and figured something like that must've happened. I called Jackie and told her the news. She turned on the television and was relaying information to me as the bus hurried towards midtown. As we left the World Trade Center, I witnessed countless men racing towards the wounded building. Instinctively, these people ran towards the danger instead of away from it. I can still remember some of their faces, all brave and resolute. I remember admiring their courage and I still do.

When I got to the office, news had just broke that the second tower had been crashed into by a second airplane. Everything was happening so fast, it was hard to process. People at the firm were all milling about -- trying to understand what was going on, glued to the news reports breaking on CNBC from the dozens of televisions that hung throughout the office. Many of the women were mournfully crying as they absorbed the information coursing from the TV's -- and I didn't feel they were scared more than the men; but we were able to hide it better.

As chaos unfolded around us, my phone rang and rang, so I picked it up. It was my obstinate client from Texas, Keith.

"Hi George, you there?"

"Yeah Keith, can you believe what's going on?"

"I see it, but I was wondering if you were in one of them buildings. I was hoping you might've been."

"Wow, did you just say that to me, you son of a bitch?"

Keith remained silent.

I continued, "do me a favor Keith and fuck off", and I hung up on him.

At around a quarter to 10am, news broke that a plane had crashed into the Pentagon. Considering we were in the third tallest building in NYC, I told my small crew that we ought to get the heck out of there. Giovanni, Dean, Eric, Nick, Chuck and myself rushed out of the building and into a panorama of panic. Not knowing where to go, we decided to walk north and away from vital targets. On our way uptown, I saw construction workers huddled around cars listening to the news being broadcasted on radio – all with stern faces and attentive eyes, expressing a combination of anger and uncertainty. Traffic lights were not being obeyed. The trains weren't working, so everyone who didn't live in Manhattan walked aimlessly throughout the city, marooned and unable to get home. We felt like sitting ducks, exposed, and could come under attack at any given moment. A little past 10am, we found out one of the towers collapsed. When I heard it, I felt a true sense of dread, like something had been stolen from me and I could never get it back. The more we walked uptown, the steeper the hills became; and every once in a while, we'd stop and peer down at the one lonely tower, smoldering and mortally wounded, yet still standing, and appreciated its strength. Hundreds of people lined the sidewalks of Harlem gawking at the strong tower, defiantly standing there without its twin; and then it fell.

The towers were gone, forever, and people in the streets were shocked to the point of obedient silence.

"Whoever did this is gonna pay," I said to Chuck.

"Damn right. George Bush is gonna nuke someone."

Stunned and dazed, we then headed back downtown on the west side and settled in at an Irish pub in midtown, where we drank beers and watched the news, taking in the destruction and the anguish that had just been inflicted upon our city. I felt extremely patriotic and wanted revenge immediately. The news reports said the culprits were of Middle Eastern descent and everyone there was in agreement that America should wage a gigantic war with whoever was responsible, as soon as possible. Saying these things made us feel better – because it gave us a break from being victims and feeling sorry for ourselves.

After many hours, the trains began to work again and I arrived home just before dark. My wife was worried sick about me, because cell phone service was out and she hadn't heard from me since the morning. We hugged and exchanged stories and went to bed that night with the windows open, admitting a gentle breeze into our bedroom that was imbued with the haunting aromas of smoke and metal. I'll always remember it, not because it was unpleasant, but because it frightened me.

Chapter IX

Immediately following the 9/11 attacks, the Federal Reserve slashed interest rates by 50 basis points to 3.00%. Ever since the year began, they had been frenetically cutting interest rates from the 6% level, admitting that their previous position of containing inflation had been a grave miscalculation. Now with the towers gone and the stock market in crisis, they had their hands full trying to stave off a full blown panic.

The economy was officially in a recession and most of the nihilists around the office were predicting a greater doom on par with the Great Depression.

The attacks caused a market closure for four days – the longest since World War I. The whole country was angered and mourning the great loss of life and a wave of patriotism spread like wild fire. On Monday, September 17th, 2001, I got up early for work, donned my favorite navy blue suit, lightly starched white shirt, and solid red tie -- and decided to board the subway that morning, instead of the express bus, so that I could ride with my fellow citizens.

As I boarded the crowded train, I was struck by the sullen mood that radiating throughout the car. Everyone wore dark funeral clothes and a somber expression – decorated with shiny America flag lapels, proudly displayed for all to bear witness. We were all brave train warriors, defiantly riding inside the underground tunnels, even though terrorists were out there – just waiting to kill us all. We didn't care. We were Americans and we weren't going to negotiate with terrorists, nor change our way of life. On that one day, we all loved riding the damned trains, in spite of how dreadful they smelled or how filthy and disgusting they appeared. They were our disgusting trains and the terrorists were not going to take them away from us.

By the time we reached downtown Brooklyn, the train was crowded shoulder to shoulder. Hardly anyone was talking and absolutely no one was laughing or showing the faintest signs of elation amidst the sea of gloomy faces that traveled in the car. I was finishing up my Tolstoy novel; but I was having a hard time getting through it with so much on my mind.

Suddenly, someone hit me hard on my American flag lapel and said in a thick Egyptian accent, "George, how the hell are you?"

It was my old colleague, Abdul.

The last time I saw Abdul was when the NYPD removed him from our offices on charges of beating on his girlfriend. After he was fired from the firm, like a locust, he hopped from firm to firm, making a mess along the way – in search of a place that cheerfully accepted locusts. Those places were indeed hard to find, which is why he bounced around so much.

Nearly shocked by Abdul's boisterous demeanor, I whispered to him, "doing well Abdul, how are you?" I didn't want to disturb my fellow compatriots.

"Good, good, good. I'm at a new firm now, very good. Fucking shit, your firm fired me for a lie, some bitch said I had hit her. It was a fucking lie."

"That's nice Abdul, say how's work?", again trying to keep the decibels at a minimum.

Speaking even louder and with the thickest Egyptian accent imaginable, he said "that bitch was a fucking whore. She lied. I don't date American girls anymore after that. They are all bitches and liars, fucking whores." He then let out a devilish laugh that rattled the train car's silence.

I physically recoiled from what he just said and quickly became worried that my fellow American flag lapel wearing compatriots might think I was in concert with this maniac, perhaps viewing him as a potential suspect for terrorist activities.

I nudged Abdul in his stomach and whispered, "hey cut it out you idiot. Don't you see everyone looking at you? They're probably gonna have you arrested at the next stop you god damned moron."

Abdul belly laughed and said "fuck them. Look, look, look, markets are gonna get killed today, yes?"

"I suppose so," I said, indifferently.

"That's good. On Monday, right before the fucking planes crashed into the buildings, I bought puts on the S&P. I'm going to make a lot of money today. I got very lucky."

"That's really great, Abdul," I mumbled with a sinking feeling in my gut. About 10 people in the car were now eagerly listening to just about everything Abdul was saying, glaring at him with suspicious eyes. I felt it was only a matter of time before some brave soul made a citizen's arrest and detained Abdul for the police to interrogate.

"Fuck this market. It's going down," said Abdul, laughing mightily. "Hey George, how's Giovanni?"

"He's doing great," I said, relieved that he changed the subject.

Shortly thereafter, my stop arrived and I quickly extricated myself from Abdul, saying 'so long', thinking I'd end up seeing him on the news that night.

When I arrived at the office, there was nothing but long faces, except for Tom's. He gestured over to me and offered me some fatherly advice: "George, today is not a day to shrink from markets. Call your clients. Get them to buy some American stocks today. We cannot let the terrorists win."

I nodded my head in agreement, but I was thinking the exact opposite. I thought what he was preparing to do was the equivalent of throwing his perfectly fine clients into a burning house that was sure to burn down. Markets were bad enough on their own; now with the added bonus of gigantic terrorist attacks on U.S. soil, taking out our skyscrapers and Pentagon, I felt confident that markets would race lower and destroy good meaning folks like Tom with fiendish violence.

"Well, George, I'll tell ya something," explained Tom – "this might not be the bottom, but I haven't asked my clients for money in over a year. Seeing how everything is down so much since then, buying now only makes me half as stupid as everyone else. I'm gonna buy some GE, Lucent and some Bank of America today. Fuck the terrorists."

"Yes, Tom, don't let them win."

"You're damned straight George."

"Hey Tom?"

"Yes George?"

"Go get them."

"You betcha."

And Tom went on using that line about being half as dumb as everyone else and got a great many of his clients to buy GE, Lucent and Bank of America that day, a day that saw the Dow lower by 700 and the Nasdaq down 7%.

As for me, I blew out of many of our speculative stocks, reducing our leverage to zero. Admittedly, many clients that I spoke to were very eager to buy the blood in the streets, which was flowing rather profusely, and I obliged them on more than one occasion; but net net, I was a seller.

By Friday morning of that first week back after 9/11, the Nasdaq hit a low of 1,387, off by more than 13% since Tom had convinced his long list of family and friends to belly dive with him into GE, Lucent, and Bank of America. I felt like a genius, or half as dumb as Tom, for avoiding the trap.

On October 7th, President Bush announced America had begun airstrikes against Al Qaeda bases in Afghanistan, declaring that 'enemies of freedom had waged war against America.' The whole country was delighted by this news and we watched the action from the comforts of our living rooms, as our space aged warplanes dropped innumerable tonnes of 'smart munitions' onto people hiding out in ancient caves.

During the early days of the Afghan war, America unleashed its latest weapon in its arsenal, the unmanned air vehicle or UAV – which was truly the star of this new and exciting war. I was enamored by this weapon of war and when I got back to the office was delighted to find out that Chase used to cover the sector when he was an analyst at the firm. He and I would converse and laugh about the sector for hours inside of his office, vigorously debating who might win the UAV arms race -- mostly uninterrupted, except for the few occasions when he needed to fire someone. After his work was done, I'd head back in there with a notepad and energetically jot down notes, which I would then pass onto clients and prospects.

The war reinvigorated my business and I was soon allocating assets into a sundry of military stocks, like General Dynamics, Alliant Tech Systems and United Industrial Corporation – the latter being a small company and the maker of the Pioneer drone – one of the stars so often featured on the nightly news reports regarding the Afghanistan war.

My clients greedily gobbled up as many shares of it as they could muster.

It was the most patriotic pitch of all time: "buy into this stock Mr. Jones and do your part in saving America from freedom hating barbarians hiding in caves."

Hardly anyone said no to me and the market helped by surging higher – vaulting 15% off the 9/11 lows.

When Halloween rolled around, Jackie and I dressed our 5 year old son as a Navy Seal, equipped with machine gun, grenades, helmet, and giant American flag sewed onto his arm sleeve. Little George was treated as a hero in Bay Ridge that Halloween and was offered copious amounts of candy for his service in wearing such a patriotic costume.

During the month of November, I expanded my menu of military stocks to include Northrop Grumman, Lockheed Martin and Raytheon. In a sense, I was like an arms dealer, peddling death and destruction for profit and I felt great doing it. I had both Dean and Eric working 'round the clock pitching new accounts, using the narrative that defense spending was about to explode to the upside. It was hard to debate the nightly news reports that discussed 'the war on terror' and possible expansion of it into other countries in the region.

In spite of this newly found passion and success, our production numbers still slumped, since defense stocks were slow movers and not really the trading type of thesis. I was building a new book and was raising a lot of new assets and it required that I be patient in the manner by which I cultivated it.

Needless to say, I was still barreling towards the bread line, burning through $5-$10,000 per month of my savings.

By Thanksgiving, the 1,387 lows on the Nasdaq were firmly in the rear view mirror – higher by 37% and everyone felt great. The Federal Reserve had cut rates to 2.00% and the market had a 1998 bottom feel to it. Who would've known that the flush out event we needed was to have madmen fly commercial airliners into skyscrapers to get the market heading higher again? The office was buzzing with energy and Tom was high like a lark, fastidiously carrying on with his clients, practically forcing them to buy more GE, Lucent, and Bank of America.

A few weeks before Christmas, Tom went over to Nick, who was casually on the phone with a client, and asked him to join him in Chase's office when he was done – and to bring his book. The past year had been hard on Nick, who was struggling to gin up business, like so many others at the firm.

Because Tom asked for him to bring his book into Chase's office, a sinister place that was used to cull brokers, Nick knew he was about to get fired.

So instead of heading into the buzz-saw to face his executioners, Nick decided to simply grab a few vital belongings, his book, and then run towards the door as fast as he could. Seeing Nick make a run for it, Tom quickly gave chase and resembled a potato with legs yelling across the boardroom in a panic, "Nick, please come back here. Nick..."

Tom was no match for Nick, who bolted out of the office, down the stairs, and finally out of the building. A clean escape.

"Can you believe this shit?", Giovanni said to me. "These sons of a bitches are killing off everyone, running them out of the office and into the streets like dogs."

"Unfuckingbelievable," I fired back.

The interminable firings continued and I often wondered how many damned brokers were left and how they kept finding new ones to get rid of.

After 15 minutes, Tom came back to the office with an expression of misery. Unlike Chase, who had ice coursing through his veins, Tom hated letting people go and took everything to heart.

"That one got away, eh Tom?", I said.

Almost in tears, Tom replied, "George, I fucking hate this business. It's just cruel, awfully cruel. Poor Nick. I only wanted to make it easier for him; now they're gonna have to mark his license and it'll be harder for him to get a new job."

"How so, Tom?"

"He left with firm property and must bring it back. You should call him up and tell him to bring the book back, otherwise they're gonna mark his license."

Having a mark on your license was the equivalent to a badge of shame. It'd stay with you for as long as you were licensed and its brand could be viewed online for the public to purview whenever they wanted.

Tom got up and labored back into Chase's office and then popped his head out and motioned to Chuck: "please come in and bring your book."

Giovanni and I looked at one another and then Chuck -- who stared at us helplessly with an expression of desperation. There was nothing we could do. For all we knew, we could've been next to be called into the executioner's office that grave afternoon.

Chuck regained his composure, grabbed his book, and walked directly into Chase's office, bravely and resolutely.

"Such a brave man," I said to Giovanni.

"Those cocksuckers. This is a shot across our bow, George. A slap in the face, firing all of our friends. We oughta to something about it, George. I'm telling ya."

"A god damned shot across our bow, Giovanni."

"That's right, George," glaring at me with bulging eyes of rage.

Inside the executioner's office, both Chase and Tom told Chuck they were very sorry, but he had to go. They kindly asked for his book of clients and told him they'd be kind enough as to let his record show he had resigned.

Chuck obstinately rejected their suggestion and valiantly fought for his job.

"What if I could double my moneyline over the next three months?"

"We're very sorry, Chuck, but our decision is final," said Chase.

"I'm not one of them, let me prove to you that I can do this."

"One of who, Chuck?", asked Tom.

"The fucking losers you guys fire every Friday."

This went on for an hour, Chuck battling hard against Chase and Tom until he was drenched in sweat; and then he made them an offer that would save his beloved job.

"What if I worked for George and Giovanni?", begged Chuck. "They'd manage my book and I'd open accounts for them."

Happy to be done with the debate, Chase acquiesced and then filled us in with the details, which we accepted.

Chuck stared down the barrel of Chase's gun and stuck his finger in it. After 6 months of pretending to work for us, we transferred Chuck's accounts back into his rep number and concluded the charade.

The latter days of 2001 turned out to be uplifting, an echo of an erstwhile brilliance in spite of the evils of the day. In the final three months of the year, markets billowed higher by 32%, off by 19% total – a rather pedestrian decline in light of the recession, millions of jobs lost, and the destruction of the World Trade Center and ongoing war on terror.

Chapter X

Markets, more or less, did nothing for the first quarter of 2002, drifting, ever so slightly lower -- like a fading dream. There was a distinct uneasiness to the decline, especially since the economy was in a tailspin and the war on terror kept us all on edge.

Every morning Chuck would rush Giovanni and me to the diner down the block for the eggs special, which was served to patrons before 11am. Sometimes, we'd get there at 11:05am; but Chuck would argue for the eggs special, blaming the restaurant's clocks or some unforeseen event that always led to Chuck being able to save 50 cents on his breakfast. These were austere times and we lived tight, no longer expecting greatness; instead, we strived for survival.

For lunch, we'd often go to three blocks down to an Italian deli for a gigantic hero stuffed with meats for about $6, or the Manhattan Chili Company for third-rate chili retailed at recessionary prices. On rare occasions, we'd visit the Grand Central Oyster Bar and sit right at the bar, never inside the actual restaurant – because we found we could get the same great clam chowder for a cheaper price. Plus, we enjoyed the pageantry of watching the chefs cook up the chowder right in front of us.

We rarely consumed alcohol during market hours, except for one time when it was a really bad day, Chuck, Giovanni and I ventured off to some dive bar for beers, got drunk, then went to a Time Square arcade for the balance of the day.

In early March of 2002, I remember gazing out of my expansive window onto Lexington Avenue, seeing the people walk by a boarded-up store front – thinking how foreboding it looked, like a relic out of the Great

Depression photos that were seared into my mind. Dean interrupted my day dream, handed me a note, and then left.

It read: "I'm an alcoholic and have been for quite some time. Off to rehab. Goodbye."

I couldn't believe what I had just read, as if it was some sort of off-color prank. Heck, Dean was barely 27, sharp as a whip, and was the best coldcaller I ever had -- and just like that, he was gone.

Months later he called us up after rehab and told us he'd been drinking at his desk from the very beginning of his employment and had picked up the addiction while away at college. We thought he was drinking grotesquely large quantities of soda; it was, but also mixed with vodka.

Just before spring arrived, Chase called me into his office to discuss 'a very small matter.'

"Hello George, I have a small favor to ask of you," said Chase, seated in a tiny office that was overflowing with scents of his flowery cologne.

"Sure, what's up?"

"As you know, our institutional desk has been expanding rapidly and we're running out of space to place new recruits. Would it be all right with you if we moved you guys into the back boardroom? We can make it comfortable for you and there's a good group of brokers back there you might like."

"Makes no difference to me, Chase," I said. "Just let me know when you want to me to go."

I knew right then and there the firm had lost confidence in us. I wasn't special anymore. I was just like everyone else, just a rep number and a production run. If that run got too small, I too could be fired and asked kindly to hand over my book of clients in exchange for being permitted to resign.

In early April, following an argument with Giovanni, Eric quit and went to work on his own at the firm. Chase asked us if he should fire him or let him try to make it on his own. He was a childhood friend of mine and I liked him, so of course I tried to help him succeed. He did not. By the summer of 2002, he left the business.

Our new work area was quiet, filled with former top producers, a ruefully oppressive place, tired, and very somber. It reminded me of a junkyard stored with yesterday's glory, stacked and rusted, awaiting to be recycled. Mostly everyone was despondent and hardly anyone worked.

The only aspirational view in that part of the office was an older gentleman named Davis, who was supremely seated in an all glass office next to us. Davis wasn't his first name, but that's what he liked to be called and always introduced himself as such: "Hello, Davis here, nice to make your acquaintance," is how he typically introduced himself. He was always tanned, probably from long hours spent on the many first rate golf courses he traversed with his very wealthy clients around the country. I often looked into Davis' office and thought "man, he has it made."

His largest client was a top executive at GE, but he spent most of his time trading his own $12 million account, probably for leisure. We often joked that the firm put Davis in the office because they couldn't bear seeing such a fine gentleman seated amidst the dregs of society in the boardroom.

Sitting directly in front of me was Roger, roughly 10 years my senior, short athletic build, dark features. During his heyday, Roger was the biggest producer at his firm, doing $3 million in annual production; now he played depression chess all day on his computer, without ever thinking about drumming up new business.

To the right of me was Mitch, one of the many managers at the firm who truly didn't give a shit about the firm. He often wished out loud we'd go bankrupt, in order to 'put him out of his misery.' Mitch had a wild mane that looked Einsteinian, jet black with touches of silver on the sides, and a thick black porn mustache to match. Once upon a time, Mitch was a top producer; now he was a low ranking manager on the dole, dispirited and melancholic. Mitch liked to complain about his wife making so much more than money than him and the fact that his house in Westport, CT was a 'fucking knockdown' and how a certain broker at the firm turned famous blogger was a 'fucking five time loser' with a 'coffee cup attached to his fucking hand.'

Giovanni sat to the left of me and a chubby man with a pony tail named Dicky sat in front of him, diagonal to me. Dicky was my favorite burnout at the firm, a former Grateful Dead roadie who once sold peanut butter and jelly sandwiches to stoners in parking lots across America. He had a soft happy round face, half Korean, half European mutt, about 5 years older than me. His true passion was the culinary arts, having went to a French culinary institute and worked in kitchens throughout Manhattan before deciding to get rich in finance.

Mitch and Dicky had a lot in common, both care free men with a certain air of sophistication to them. I often thought Mitch was a future version of Dicky and whenever I told him that, Dicky would say "pfff, whatever dude."

Dicky and I became great friends and he often dragged me to fine dining cafes and restaurants in the city, in spite of my demands for a more frugal experience. He was easy in almost every regard, with exception to the food he ate.

Our favorite spot was the Palm II Steakhouse on West 45th and Second Avenue, a smaller version of its sister restaurant Palm I, which was located downtown. It had an intimate dining room, brimming with history. The walls were completely covered with murals depicting caricatures of famous celebrities with funny quotes next to their faces, some of them were autographed. Other than that, it was a rather plain, almost dingy, haunt; but the steaks were second to none and we liked it just fine.

One afternoon, we went to Palm II, sat down, and ordered two 2 ½ inch thick rib eyes, heavily salted, lightly peppered – served medium rare. Dicky was authoritative with the waiters – but treated them well, and tipped them even better.

"Excuse me, Sir," Dicky beckoned the waiter, waiving his right hand in the air.

The waiter hurried over to us and asked how he could be of service; to which Dicky replied, "I'd like you to bring me a few ingredients so that I could make my own steak sauce, tableside."

"I will try to accommodate you best I can Sir."

"Okay then, this is what I need, if you would be so kind. Bring me a saucer of cocktail sauce, some Tobasco, Dijon mustard, and Worcester – and if you have it, bring some horseradish."

"I believe I have all of those ingredients. Would that be all Sir?", asked the courteous waiter with a hurried expression scribbled across his hard featured face.

"That'll be just fine. Thank you," said Dicky.

"What the heck is that for?", I asked.

"For the steak, George. You mustn't waste a perfectly good steak without having a great condiment to go with it. Don't tell me you prefer ketchup or A1 sauce?", asked Dicky with a concerned look on his face.

"Who me? Never," I said, slightly defensive since I liked a good dose of ketchup and now felt guilty about it.

"This is my favorite way to eat a steak," exclaimed Dicky. "If you're going to spend $50 on a steak, you might as well have the proper condiment to go with it."

Regaining my gusto, I said, "I suppose so Dicky. But usually I just eat the damn steak without any sauce. You know, some people, steak aficionados especially, would get very mad at you for sullying an otherwise fine piece of beef with some cheap carnivale sauce made tableside."

Dicky laughed and said "believe me, I know. I used to work in a steakhouse and the kitchen staff hated requests like that, which is why I asked for the ingredients to make the sauce myself at the table. The worst was when a customer asked for a steak to be cooked well done. We'd just throw it in the microwave and serve it steaming hot.

We had no respect for people who didn't respect a good piece of meat."

Dicky continued, "some people have no respect for food. Ya know, George?" I agreed and then Dicky took a healthy sip of water and started to butter a hot roll that had just been placed at the table and said, "but, you'll see, George, it's a fine sauce and it's quite good."

We were seated next to a window facing 2nd Avenue. It was a sublime spring day in the city, with scores of people milling about enjoying the pleasant weather. Along with the bread, our waiter delivered a bottle of Bordeaux. Dicky had chosen a 1998 because he said it was the best year for Bordeaux in the 90s and it was his favorite region in the world for red wine, especially paired with great steaks. I trusted his recommendation and gulped my first glass down like it was fruit punch.

This alarmed Dicky.

"George, you're supposed to aerate the wine, swirl it in the glass, and sip is slowly. Look, hold the glass at about a 45 degree angle and stick your nose in the glass and fully breathe in the scents, take a sip, and then exhale out from your nose. Here, take some more and give it a sincere try," asked Dicky in a scholarly manner.

I stuck my nose into the glass like a rube and flatly said "It smells just like wine."

Dismissing what I had just said, Dicky continued, "let the wine sit on your palate for a good five seconds before you swallow. Try to detect some of the aromas on the nose before drinking. Okay George?"

He then picked up his glass and expertly swirled the wine rapidly in his goblet, a skill that I hadn't mastered yet, and stuck his nose so far into the glass I swore he took a dip. With a graceful air of sophistication, Dicky greedily breathed in the aromas of the velvety red wine and then took a measured sip.

"For example, with this wine I smell some rocks, fresh cut grass, a little cognac, and sheep's butt," he declared.

"Yummy, sounds delicious, Dicky. Do you drink wine out from the ass of sheep much?"

"Right now I do," he replied, giving out a whimsical laugh.

"Seriously George, when you're drinking wine, especially good wine like this, you need to savor it and try to discover all of the intricacies of the flavor profile. If you can do that, then and only then will you begin to enjoy wine."

"Indeed, I'll have to give it some practice then, eh?"; raising my glass, I took another hideous swig and gulped it down.

"Hey Dicky, look who's passing by, Giovanni, Paul and Chuck. Should I invite them in for lunch?"

"Sure, why not?"

As I ran outside to intercept my friends, who were probably en route to fetch a hero from a cheap Italian deli, Dicky motioned to our waiter to make seating arrangements for new guests.

"Hey fuckers," I shouted out onto a crowded Second Avenue.

Chuck looked back first, and then all three greeted me; and I extended an invitation to lunch, to which they happily accepted.

The wait staff quickly connected two tables to ours, placed heavy silverware, thick white napkins, three glasses of water, and some empty wine glasses on them; and then we all sat down.

"So, what did you ladies order?", quizzed Chuck.

"Steak moron, what the hell else would we order in a steakhouse?", I replied.

"I know that, asshole," said Chuck. "Anything else?"

Dicky proffered some advice and said, "you should try the asparagus and the home fries. They're quite good."

Both Paul and Chuck ordered rib eyes with a side of home fries, and Giovanni asked for the NY Strip – because he wanted something smaller and because he wasn't too hungry.

The sides came out first and Dicky ordered another 4 bottles of his favorite Bordeaux and everyone drank heartily and enjoyed the home fries and asparagus. Paul was especially fond of the asparagus and began to hog it for himself, but was interrupted by Chuck, who said "save some for us, you asparagi pig" – violently sticking his fork into a row of heavily seasoned asparagus.

The restaurant was thrumming with conversation and the sounds of people eating, forks dropping on top of plates, and the incidental clattering of wine glasses against expensive silverware. It was about 1:30pm and markets were likely doing a great deal and clients were probably pestering our assistants to speak with us – but we were busy at the Palm II, awaiting our steaks, enjoying each other's company.

"Hey Dicky, tell them about that luncheon we were invited to last week and what you did", I said.

"Oh, that, yes of course. See, George and I were invited to one of those promotional luncheons from the CEO of Immune Response --"

Paul interrupted and said "I know that company. A client of mine owns the stock. How'd it go?"

"I'll tell you in a moment, hang on", Dicky said excitedly, taking a generous sip of his wine, without sticking his nose in it first.

"So, we get there and it's about 12 of us, George and I being the only ones under 50 years old and the CEO shakes my hand." Dicky then took a moment to laugh and placed his hand on his head as if to warn us the punchline was coming, "and I felt absolutely dreadful, truly awful, and was really drowsy because I had just taken a lot of Benadryl and my eyes were bloodshot red. Weren't they George?"

"You looked like vampire", I said, chewing wildly on a piece of hot bread.

Dicky continued, "so I said to him, while shaking his hand with a firm grip, 'pardon my disposition, I caught a dose of poison oak last weekend while picking wild mushrooms on my property upstate and I'm loaded up with anti-histamines.'"

Everyone began to laugh and Paul nearly spit out a mouthful of wine onto the table.

"Hang on guys, it gets better," I said. "Continue Dicky."

"The CEO quickly recoiled and stood up and said, 'good God, if you have poison oak, why in the hell are you shaking my hand?' I looked up at him and said, 'relax, you'll be fine pal, you have immune response, don't you?'"

"Oh shit, I bet he was speechless after that, huh Dicky?", said Chuck.

I chimed in, "after a few minutes the con artist settled in and figured if we could buy enough stock from him, it'd be worth the dose of poison oak."

Everyone nodded in agreement, knowing full well that those sort of luncheons, which were very common in the brokerage circuit, were all shams.

"And Paul, you should tell your client to sell the stock. They're likely to do a secondary soon, once the CEO is able to do enough luncheons to get the stock a little higher."

"Thanks, George, I'll give him a call later on."

The wait staff began to hover around us, catering to our every whim. It must had had something to do with the fact that we were the only fools in there getting drunk, ordering bottle after bottle of Bordeaux. They told us the steaks were nearly done, but we didn't care too much since the conversation was good and the mood was delightful. Being the good waiters they were, they brought us another three baskets of warm bread with warm butter, and then cleaned the breadcrumbs off our tables expertly and without much commotion. I grabbed some pumpernickel, lathered some butter onto it, and ate the whole piece in two giant bites.

"What sort of wine is this, George?" asked Giovanni.

"Oh this? This is sheep's butt, imported from the farms of France, 1998. Can't you tell?"

Paul laughed and said, "you know what, it does have a little sheep's butt quality to it."

Dicky grinned while skillfully swirling his wine in his goblet.

Chuck was looking around the restaurant and said "hey, look who's over there in the corner eating. It's John McEnroe. "

"To hell with John McEnroe," Giovanni said while letting out a boisterous laugh. "I don't like tennis."

Dicky chimed in and said he once played tennis with John, which drew cynical laughter. Dicky often told outlandish stories that we called 'Dickyisms', also known as lies. However, some of his stories, as crazy as they sounded, actually checked out – which threw us off-guard. It was part of Dicky's eccentric manner. One of the more absurd stories he once told me was the time he drove from Texas to NY in a single day. I did the math on my calculator and said, "you'd need to drive at an average rate of 66mph without stopping for gas for 24 hours straight."

"Fucking impossible," I said.

He simply smiled and said, "for you."

Our waiter appeared out of nowhere, balancing three large dishes of steaks with his right hand and another with this left. Giovanni's NY Strip was brought over by another waiter and everyone had been served.

Dicky offered everyone a spoonful of his custom made steak sauce, which I enjoyed quite a bit. I cut into the thick crust of the rib eye with barbarous qualities, ripping through the charred exterior and into the juicy meat, which was dripping with flavor. I took some of Dicky's sauce and placed it onto my plate, dipped my meat into it, and then devoured it. After that, I washed it down with a little Bordeaux, and repeated the process until nothing was left. I've always found eating steak to be somewhat of a ritualistic experience, especially amongst other men, an ancient savagery that brought out the predator in me. When done in the proper setting, like a fine steakhouse, I found it to be a very manly thing to do.

Paul said to me, "hey George, remember that time at the old firm when that Russian stockbroker was found passed out in the bathroom with a heroin needle in his arm?"

"How could I forget?"

Dicky said, "you've got to tell us that story."

I continued, "I just started out in the business on my own and in comes a new broker Ivan. He sat right next to me and looked disheveled, very nervous, and wore run-down shirts that needed a good ironing. He plopped down an enormous amount of leads on his desk and told me they were all his clients."

"How many leads, George?", asked Chuck.

"About 500, maybe more," I said. "So, one day he takes break from calling his clients, who by the way were all hanging up on him because, obviously, they weren't his clients; and Nick comes running into the boardroom with his bright green eyes bulging out of his head and said, 'Ivan the Russian is passed out dead in the bathroom with a fucking heroin needle stuck in his arm.'"

"Who, our Nick?", asked Giovanni.

"Yep."

"Oh my God, so what happened next, was he dead?", asked Chuck.

"No, but what happened next shall forever be seared into my mind as a metaphor of how dreadful those stockbrokers were."

Paul had a smile from ear to ear, anticipating the punchline that he already knew.

"Within seconds," I continued, "the brokers in the office processed the potential demise of one of their own, looked at Ivan's giant stack of leads resting on his desk, and then plundered it like common thieves, taking them all. After they were done taking the leads on his desk, Nick, through brute force, jimmied open his file cabinet, pillaging all of the contents inside of it."

"What fine marauding pirates you worked with," posited Dicky.

We all laughed at poor Ivan's expense, drank some more wine, and then laughed some more.

"About a week later, after getting fired of course, Ivan came back for his belongings and asked me what had happened to his leads. I didn't have the heart to tell him the truth, so I just shrugged my shoulders and said, 'I'm sure they'll show up somewhere and the firm will contact you when they do.' And that was that."

"A fine story," said Dicky. He continued, "on the subject of Nick, I once sat next to him and heard him say some of the most abhorrent things known to mankind to his poor clients."

"Like what?", I asked.

"Well, this one time," said Dicky, "a client called him up during the very worst days of 2001 and asked for his account balance, to which Nick replied 'what account balance, Bob? Your account is zero; what the heck are you talking about?' The client shot back and said, 'but Nick, I had $300,000 in the account in there just a short time ago' and Nick replied 'Bob, that was like a thousand years ago', so flippantly, so nonchalantly, and then hung up the phone."

"And to make matters worse," he continued, "I asked Nick after he had hung up the phone what it was all about and how much the client had with him before getting zeroed out -- and Nick just looked at me like he was telling me the time and said '3 million, poof, all gone.'"

"Wow, that's fucked up," I said. "Sometimes I wonder why I entered this business."

"Because it's the best business in the world, George!", shouted Giovanni, sporting a giant smile.

"I'll drink to that," I said; and then we all raised our wine glasses in honor of that statement and clinked them in the middle of the table.

We were done eating around 2:30pm. The bill came and it was $1,450, not including the tip.

"Not bad," said Paul while reviewing the receipt over his spectacles.

Chuck grabbed it from Paul and then began combing over it like a stingy accountant working on Christmas Eve.

"Ah, ha, we only had 7 bottles of wine. They charged us for 8," he declared with an air of gotcha in his voice.

"Well, actually, George and I had one before you came," said Dicky.

"Ok, so let's subtract that from the bill. No sense in the rest of us paying for it," cried Chuck.

"Quit being such a jerkoff," Giovanni cried out.

He grabbed the bill, called the waiter over to the table and handed him his card and said, "charge this to my card please."

"Dude, I can't let you do that. It's too much," I said to Giovanni.

He ignored me and insisted on paying for the feast.

"Next time we go out, Chuck is paying," Giovanni said while letting out a violent laugh. Chuck grinned as if to say, "fat chance in hell." We all let out some more festive laughter and then thanked him for his generosity. After washing up in the bathroom, we headed out.

As we left the dark cavernous venue of the Palm II and into the NYC streets, my eyes were blinded by a magnificent sunshine casting onto 2nd Avenue. "It doesn't get better than this," I thought to myself, looking at my young friends all merry and content. On the way back to the office, both Paul and Chuck met some young ladies and started conversing with them. The rest of us headed back to our gilded offices, back into the frying pan of a market that had produced nothing but plain misery and sharp heartache for the past two years.

We spent the rest of the day watching the market, making small talk, and drinking copious amounts of coffee.

Chapter XI

On a sleepy afternoon in May, 2002, a small army had invaded our firm. At the head of a train of 10 young brokers was their leader. His name was Marcus and at 6'4", 250lbs, he towered over his minions. He had a dark complexion, husky build, with tight curls lightly resting on his head, which resembled black strands of spiral macaroni.

"Who the fuck are these losers?", cried an especially curmudgeon Mitch, as the convoy of new brokers barreled through the boardroom.

Our firm had just hired Marcus and paid him a large sum of money to defect from his previous firm, rumored to be in the high six figures. To accommodate Marcus and his 10 coldcallers, they gave him Steve's old office and the one next to it. Marcus had them knock down the walls to connect the two and he situated himself in the large open space like a King.

To simply say Marcus was our top producer at the time would do injury to how important he was back then. During a time when the other top producers barely broke $30,000 in monthly commissions, Marcus was doing $250,000 with ease. His secret? He simply bet against stocks and shorted them; it was like shooting fish in a barrel. Most of us avoided shorting stocks because we felt the market had bottomed and could not trade much lower. Marcus didn't believe in such aspirational thinking, and instead, put his money where his mouth was -- betting against American prosperity – hoping it'd burn to the ground.

He placed enormously large bets against stocks, all heavily margined, without fear: 300,000 shares of AMZN at the lows, betting on it going even lower – and it did. Selling short 500,000 shares of EBAY – seeing it trade down $10 – and then covering it for massive profits and commissions. Marcus only took 2-3 positions at a time and sometimes he'd do zero trades for the month – idling himself while his positions worked out. But when he covered his shorts, the gains were enormous and his commissions were tremendous.

He never fraternized with any of us and barely made eye contact. Whenever he went out for a smoke or for some food, he was ensconced by his coldcallers, who fawned over him like he was their Caesar.

"Can you believe this guy?", said Giovanni – referring to Marcus and his small army of coldcallers that just passed by us.

"He's a fucking loser," said Mitch. "I bet Tom is having a fucking fit managing him."

"Tom is his manager?", I asked. "I didn't know that."

"Yep," replied Mitch. "And when that fucking guy blows up, he's gonna take Tom with him to the NASD, so they could both lose their licenses."

"What do you mean?", asked Giovanni.

"That fucking guy is placing $5 million accounts into one fucking short position, banging clients out for maximum commissions, and no one is saying a word to him about it."

"Why is that?", I asked.

Mitch looked over at me and whispered, "because this fucking firm is gonna go under and they need people like fucked face over there to keep it afloat."

"Oh, come on Mitch," said Giovanni. "You're just being a nihilistic fucktard. The firm isn't going under."

Mitch chuckled to himself, got up, and then walked away to fetch a snack from the vending machines.

Marcus always dressed in dark suits, but often neglected to sport a tie – which was against the firm's strict dress code; but they never bothered him with small things like that. But as the market started to nosedive lower in the summer of 2002 and Marcus' power levels increased, he became bold, even crass, and it started to show in the manner he appeared at the office.

By July of 2002, markets were rolling lower on a daily basis and the cumulative losses since the bubble burst was in excess of $7.7 trillion. The Federal Reserve was powerless and unemployment was at an 8 year high, and Marcus' power was at an all-time high. It was basketball season and Marcus began showing to work clad in terry cloth sweat suits, gigantic gold chains around his neck, with basketball jerseys and shoes to match. One afternoon he appeared in a sleeveless Lakers jersey and Air Jordan sneakers, on a Tuesday, which caused Tom to spaz out and confront him. I bore witness to it and remember exactly what was said.

Tom was hard at work, analyzing some mutual fund, when he saw Marcus pass by dressed like a basketball player. I saw his eyes light up and he immediately called out, "say Marcus, can I talk to you for a moment?"

Marcus turned around to look at who dared to interrupt his gait. He spied Tom and slowly walked over to him.

When he reached Tom, he towered over him and looked twice his height; but that didn't bother Tom – who was both brave and resolute.

Tom said, "Marcus, I got to tell ya, ya can't come in here looking like that. Clients could be in the office and it simply isn't professional. Please, don't come in here dressed in shorts and a sleeveless sports jersey for God's sake."

Marcus looked bored while Tom rambled on and dismissively, replied, "look, I don't have to listen to anything you say and I don't answer to you, only the boss. If you have a problem with it, go talk to Mike." And he walked away.

Tom stood there for 10 seconds, processing what Marcus had just said to him, and then quickly walked over to Mike's office to lodge a complaint. Marcus came to work for the remainder of the week dressed like a basketball player, each day increasing with both egregious audacity and inelegance, which led to Tom resigning his post as manager at the firm. Apparently, Mike sided with his top producer, who enjoyed the superficialities of summer street attire, rather than the austere Tom – who felt suits and ties were going to keep the lights on.

On July 10th, 2002, the Nasdaq broke below the 9/11 lows of 1,387 – unleashing a storm of pessimism and helplessness onto Wall Street. The idea of breaching those lows was foreboding and it was symbolic of the ongoing war on terror. Within a fortnight, stocks were racing lower without brakes – hitting the unthinkable level of 1,206 on July 19th. In a little less than 2 ½ years, the Nasdaq had shed 75% of its value – reducing most tech stocks to absolute saw dust, replete with hundreds of bankruptcies and shattered dreams.

By October 9th, 2002, the drudgery of work felt like a ludicrous waste of time. It was, unquestionably, a living and breathable hell -- a tortuous milieu where people went to feel bad and lose large sums of money. There wasn't any place to hide, as the Nasdaq hit new lows of 1,114 – down roughly 4,000 points since the ebullient days of 2000. By that time, Marcus had reached God-like status, producing more than the 15 top producers combined.

"Jesus Christ, someone needs to stop that man; he's ruling over this firm with an iron fist now," complained Giovanni, as Marcus coursed by with his army.

"Someone needs to end him," said Mitch dryly, and we didn't know if he was serious or not.

Things got so bad at our firm even Davis was kicked out of his office and tossed into the junkyard with the rest of us. It was one of the saddest sights a man could ever see, distinguished Davis sitting there, looking like the CEO of General Electric, right next to some piker cold calling old ladies for IRA accounts.

"It's not right you know, kicking poor Davis out into the cold, gray, boardroom like that," I said to Giovanni.

"It's a damn shame. Just two years ago, Davis approached me and asked me to be his male secretary, answer his phones, to place trades for him while he was away on the golf course. I laughed at him and said 'get the fuck out of here Davis, I'm doing $250,000 per month.'"

"Yeah, he had an innocent sense of entitlement about him. That's for sure. Now look at him," both of us glanced over and took a hard look at Davis. "He looks terrible."

"What the fuck is he wearing anyway?", Giovanni quizzed. "Are those furry pants or some shit?"

"No, Giovanni. Those are corduroys and it's a damn shame. Davis would never be caught dead wearing those rancid pants when he was in his office."

"Poor Davis," Giovanni declared. "We'll drink to his death tonight."

One afternoon Chuck was outside of Marcus' office and overheard him pitching a client on speakerphone.

"Larry, we're gonna sell short some Dell Computer, okay?"

"Sure," said Larry.

"Listen to me," Marcus exclaimed. "I am crushing this market like no one else. All of the brokers at my firm are starving to death, fucking their clients with mammoth-sized losses. You hear me? I'm in here like a fucking God, knocking down walls, tossing other brokers to the side like wilted pieces of lettuce."

"Wow, that's great Marcus," replied Larry, impressed by Marcus' accomplishments. "Listen Marcus, I appreciate all of the money you've made me, especially at time when all of my other brokers are losing me money. But there's no need to spell it out for me like that."

Marcus ignored what his client had just said, probably because he didn't give a shit.

Marcus pressed: "that's exactly what I wanted to talk to you about. I want all of your other accounts. You fucking owe me and I will not take no for an answer."

"Well --"

Marcus interrupted, "I'm not done Larry. Do you know why I can do this? Do you know why I do not accept no for an answer? Any idea?"

"No, I don't," answered a puzzled Larry. "Why Marcus?"

Marcus then stood up, took in a healthy amount of air, placed his hands flat on the table, leaned over and yelled as loud as he could into the speakerphone: "BECAUSE I'M GHETTO FABOLOUS THAT'S WHY."

And then he hung up the damn phone, without even waiting for a response. He called his assistant and barked at her to overnight Larry three account transfer forms and then proceeded to call his other clients and he'd repeat the whole routine until the day was done.

Chuck recounted this story to anyone who'd listen to it, but a lot of people had a hard time believing it. But for those that did, Marcus was then known as "Ghetto Fabulous" and we began to see the rap music trailing just behind him as he traversed through the firm.

Ghetto Fabulous' time at the firm ended in early 2003, after Chase spied him in the front of the building smoking a blunt filled with marijuana, mid-afternoon.

When Mike heard about this, he visited Ghetto Fab's office, hoping to clear the air. He peered into his office and told him what he had heard, practically begging for an answer that would assuage his concerns. But markets were racing higher and Ghetto Fab's short positions were getting obliterated, just as Mitch predicted, and he was in a very sour mood. He shot daggers at Mike, bellowing out, "yeah, I smoked a blunt, so the fuck what? Now do me a favor and get the fuck out of my office. I've got work to do."

Needless to say, Ghetto Fab overestimated his power level and was terminated on the spot. We never heard from him again. But I'm almost certain he is doing quite well.

Chapter XII

As the last few months of 2002 fell into the abyss, our client base was being decimated by account transfers. Giovanni and I tried the best that we could to hold clients in – but we still got hit with about 5 per week. Due to the destructive market conditions, I focused my efforts on fixed income, preferred stocks, and anything that didn't drop in value. It was during this time that mutual fund salesmen visited our offices with principle guaranteed funds – hoping to raise assets from our clients by offering a guarantee of principle. Truth is, clients would've be much better off putting their money in the bank or under a mattress than in gimmicky funds with capped upsides.

The losses were interminable and I made a promise to never buy tech stocks again, seeing how grisly of an effect they had on my life. I was out of savings, tapping credit cards again, and my wife had just told me she was pregnant and expecting in April.

Our monthly gross production sunk to under $20,000, mostly supported by my unyielding efforts in raising new money, trying desperately to turn things around. There wasn't any trading being done – because no one trusted the market rallies.

After the new year, I invited Giovanni to Pret a Manger for lunch and to discuss our business. The winds were especially strong that day and the sidewalks were dusted with snow and the streets blanketed by filthy slush, which made walking around the city a chore.

"Some fucking day, ha?", I said to Giovanni, as we skipped over a large mound of snow adjacent to waste bin overflowing with trash.

"Tell me about it. I can't wait to move out of this city and head back to Florida. I'll tell ya George, these New York City winters are brutal and I don't want to live here for the rest of my life. Enough about me. I'm getting old. What's on your mind?"

"It's about our business."

"What about it?"

"It's not working."

"I know."

"I haven't bothered you about my problems Giovanni, but they're mounting. Jackie and I have another baby on the way –"

"Congratulations," cheered Giovanni, pressing my hand and giving me a light pat on my back.

"Thank you."

I continued, "I blew all of my money in the market and on an array of wasteful things that I wish I could undo, but I can't. You've been a great partner and I appreciate all that you brought to the table, but I need to go out on my own again. If I'm gonna fail, I have to do it on my terms."

"I figured this was coming," said Giovanni solemnly. "I know I haven't put my full efforts into the business lately. But I haven't been feeling well and the market, well, the market isn't a very happy place now. "

"I know."

We entered the sandwich shop and walked over to a wall filled with endless array of already made sandwich's – neatly tucked away in small cubby holes. We both grabbed the turkey thanksgiving sandwich, some iced green tea, and paid for our food.

As we walked over to a vacated table, Giovanni said, "don't worry, George. Things will turn around and you'll catch the next wave – you always do. You're only 26 for crying out loud. You'll be fine."

"I know," I said, "but I feel much older. These past few years have aged me, sapped me of my innocence and made me cynical. The market topped a little more than 2 years ago, but it feels like a decade."

I changed the subject with some lighter small talk, and ten minutes later we finished our lunch and left. On the walk back to the office, skipping around pools of icy slush, dodging speeding yellow cabs, Giovanni asked me to give him a list of the accounts I wanted; and I did so later that afternoon.

The partnership had ended, and we were still good friends, but it was different. I was on my own again, trapped in a corner, in a fight against my worst enemy.

Fin.

Please leave a 5 star review on Amazon – it helps towards financing the Orbital Space Cannon (OSC) project, designed for offensive purposes only.

Now that you've read this, shouldn't you read part 1 of this story? I get it, you got it backwards, but it's a fine story and you'll like it very much.

Indeud.

Made in the USA
San Bernardino, CA
24 March 2018